"Profoundly eerie and comprehensive, this book is one wild ride through the dark side of the Sunshine State!"

Tamrah Aeryn, Florida singer-songwriter

****

"Chad and Terry's book, **The Florida Road Guide to Haunted Locations,** *conjures memories and goose bumps while reading about some of Florida's great haunts. Definitely good fun and a hair-raising read."*

Douglas Cifers, Publisher, *Florida Monthly* magazine

****

"This series is a must-have for travelers who want to be scared by something other than motion master rides and animatronic dinosaurs. Investigators Chad Lewis and Terry Fisk probe the creepiest legends and little-known haunts. They tell you where to go, how to get there, and what you might expect to see—if you dare!"

Editors of RoadsideAmerica.com

THE
FLORIDA
ROAD GUIDE
TO
HAUNTED
LOCATIONS

THE
FLORIDA
ROAD GUIDE
TO
HAUNTED
LOCATIONS

By Chad Lewis & Terry Fisk

UNEXPLAINED
Research Publishing Company
A Division of Unexplained Research LLC

The Florida Road Guide to Haunted Locations
by Chad Lewis and Terry Fisk

Unexplained Research Publishing Company
A Division of Unexplained Research LLC
P.O. Box 2173, Eau Claire, WI 54702-2173
Email: info@unexplainedresearch.com
www.unexplainedresearch.com

Publisher's Cataloging-in-Publication
(Provided by Quality Books, Inc.)

Lewis, Chad.
    The Florida road guide to haunted locations / by Chad
Lewis & Terry Fisk.
    p. cm.
    Includes index.
    LCCN 2008923703
    ISBN-13: 978-0-9798822-2-7
    ISBN-10: 0-9798822-2-2

    1. Haunted places--Florida--Guidebooks. 2. Ghosts--
Florida--Guidebooks. 3. Legends--Florida--Guidebooks.
4. Florida--Guidebooks.   I. Fisk, Terry. II. Title.

BF1472.U6L49 2008   133.1'09759
                    QBI08-600097

Cover Design: Terry Fisk
Back Cover Photo: Rob Mattison

DEDICATION

I dedicate this book to the memory of my nephew Sean Lewis, who guided me around Florida on an adventurous skunk ape expedition.

—Chad

Dedicated to Joe, Tamrah Aeryn, and Marqaux Alexander.

—Terry

TABLE OF CONTENTS

4 - Southeast Florida   185

5 - Southwest Florida   237

PREFACE

Corrections. Although we have made every effort to be certain this road guide is reliable and accurate, things inevitably change and errors are made. We appreciate it when readers contact us so we can revise future editions of the book.

Updates. If you have a paranormal experience at one of these locations, please report it to us. We recommend that you keep a journal, carefully recording dates, times, locations, and what happened.

Additions. Due to lack of space, many locations had to be left out the book. We do intend to publish a second volume. Please write and let us know of any Florida locations that you feel should have been included in this travel guide.

Warning. Be respectful of both the living and the dead. Several communities have had problems with people who go to these locations only to party and cause mischief. Cemeteries have been desecrated; private property has been vandalized; grounds have been littered; and buildings have been broken into.

If you do decide to check out any of the locations for yourself, please make sure that you have permission if it is private property and obey all applicable laws. Under most ordinances, cemeteries are only open from sunrise to sunset.

We will not be held responsible for any persons who decide to conduct their own investigations or for those who choose to break laws.

Disclaimer. The places listed in the book have neither been proved nor disproved to be haunted. Their inclusion in the book is based on the anecdotal reports we have received from numerous individuals. This book is for reference purposes only.

FOREWORD

My interest in Florida's history and folklore began many years ago in rural Seminole County sitting on Granny Hawkins' front porch listening to her never-ending collection of ghost stories. This was the Old Florida, where gators, palmettos, and the absence of air conditioning were a part of life, long before the Sunshine State became famous for theme parks and notorious for over-development. It is through Granny Hawkins, my maternal grandmother, that I trace my family lineage back ten generations in Florida, which makes me a living oddity in a population of mostly transplants and tourists. My ancestral connection to the state's past destined me to become a Florida historian and eventually a folklorist. All folklore has a bit of history; the trick is in separating fact from fiction. For most fans of the paranormal, a ghost story supported by historical fact is far more intriguing than one lacking substance. That's what I like about *The Florida Road Guide to Haunted Locations,* in which Chad Lewis and Terry Fisk offer readers both lore and history, plus clear directions to haunted locations.

Granny did not have Chad and Terry's guide book, nor did she have any modern electronic gadgets like television, computers, cell phones or iPods for entertainment; instead, she preferred sitting peacefully in her rickety, old rocking chair, "pondering nature," or as we call it today, "meditating." Actually, I believe she was communing with the dearly departed because Granny was a genuine medium, which had nothing to do with her size and everything to do with talking to dead folks. I was about six years old when I was introduced to Spiritualism. I tagged along with my mother and grandmother to a séance in Cassadaga, a town where all residents are mediums. Normally, a six-year-old would be bored in the company of a bunch of adults, but not at this place, especially when they demonstrated automatic writing. That was over fifty years ago, but I can still recall how a piece of chalk, unaided by human hands, scribbled a spiritual message on a slate. Needless to say, seeing weird stuff like that when you're only six is enough to cause anyone to believe in ghosts. Was it really a chalk-writing spirit? I don't know and can only report what I saw, but if you're a fan of the afterlife and haven't been to Cassadaga, you'll find the directions in this book. However, if you spend the night in the hotel there, you might meet Arthur, the cigar smoking gentleman staying in Room 22. My advice is to pay him no mind; he's dead.

As a boy, nothing was as exciting as spending evenings on my grandmother's unscreened porch, "swattin' skeeters" in the dim light of a kerosene lamp while she spun yarns about Florida's "haints"—a Southern term for "things that are best left alone." Granny always warned us to "be careful messing with the dead." I don't know exactly what she meant, but her warning still echoes in my head whenever I participate in a paranormal investigation. Most of Granny's yarns are now lost to history, except for what was fused forever in my impressionable mind as a youngster. One story, a favorite of mine, had to do with an apparition frequently seen prior to 1900 by residents of Lemon Bluff, a riverside settlement in Volusia County on the St. Johns River. The subject specter of this yarn was an old woman who on moonlit nights would rise from the depths of the river. Described as drenched in mud, and perhaps with a bullfrog sitting on her head, this ghostly old hag would float eerily up to people's back porches where she drank from their water buckets. After quenching her ghoulish thirst, she would return to the river, vanishing into its dark water. I always wondered why a ghost would need to drink water.

Allegedly, the apparition in Granny's story was a woman who had drowned in the river. In reality, historical documentation is severely lacking in this case, therefore, consider it just another ghost yarn. On the other hand, Florida has numerous places where weird stuff has been experienced by a string of witnesses and recorded on electronic instruments by paranormal investigators. One such place is Ashley's, a local eatery in Rockledge known for its poltergeist activity. It's a place where dishes fly off shelves, salt and pepper shakers move across table tops, lights turn off and on, and customers frequently report being touched or pushed by unseen hands. Ashley's management is very open about their haunting and has even included a narrative about the strangeness on their menu cover. Over the years I have hosted a couple of television documentaries filmed at Ashley's, participated in a paranormal investigation of the place, and even wrote a novel titled, *Ashley's Shadow*, so I was very pleased to find that Chad and Terry have included this legendary restaurant in this book. Although this is not a restaurant guide, I have dined at most of the haunted eateries mentioned in this book and the food is always good. I know that's off topic, but I seem to work up a haunting appetite when thinking about ghosts.

Any book about Florida ghosts should include St. Augustine, the nation's Ancient City. It was here in 1513 that Ponce de Leon first set foot on Florida soil. The actual settlement was founded in 1565, which means St. Augustine is pushing toward 500 years of occupation. That's plenty of time to rack up a lot of dead folks, so it's no wonder the place is overrun with ghosts. It's also overrun with tourists who, unlike ghosts, drive cars and take up all the parking spaces. Chad and Terry have highlighted the city's best haunted sites and stories. Yeah, they missed a few mundane ones, like that two story house on Cordova Street where, "A light is seen in the upstairs window at midnight and some say a woman died there on her wedding night." I always cringe when I hear, "some people say this and that..." My question is, who are "some people" referenced in such yarns? And where's the proof someone really died there? Show me the census records or obituary or something. You're probably like me. I want a little proof that something really happened in the first place before moving on to checking out spirit stuff. Otherwise we'd just be on a wild goose chase...er, make that, wild ghost chase. Instead, Chad and Terry have focused on haunted places backed-up with history and witness experiences.

FOREWORD

Ghosts are good business for St. Augustine, as evident from its nine operating ghost tours, including one that escorts guests to all the haunted pubs. It's a great tour because at each stop you can have a drink. By the end of the tour almost every guest will have seen a spirit and some are so frightened they can hardly stand up. Ghost tours can be a fun way to spend the evening and, from Key West to Pensacola, there's something like thirty-eight operating in Florida. The downside to ghost tours is being crammed together in a group and forced to keep pace with the guide. Another problem, from my observation as a historian, is some of the newer tours seem to be making up stories. Of course, if you're a tourist from out of town, you wouldn't know if a tale is true or not. I have a better suggestion: use this *Road Guide to Florida's Haunted Locations*. It has all the information you need—the stories, history and directions. The best part is you'll save money and will be able to take your own time exploring haunted places.

This should be the only guide ever needed by Florida ghostbusters. Speaking of ghost hunting, in 2004 I spent the night in St. Augustine's Castillo de San Marcos with Florida's leading paranormal investigative group, the Spookhunters, based in Orlando. They have the uncanny ability to get into places that are off limits to other groups, like investigating a haunted launch pad at Kennedy Space Center. They are well-equipped with all types of sophisticated technology from EMF [electromagnetic field] detectors to thermal imaging devices to contraptions for recording EVPs [electronic voice phenomena] and the most high tech of all, Ouija Boards. Basically, they'll use anything if there's the slightest chance of detecting a ghost, and they've used these things on investigations in nine states. Now there's something a little weird about the Spookhunters; it's their founder and leader, Owen Sliter. His trademark is his bright orange ghost busters jumpsuit and he doesn't believe in ghosts. He's called America's Skeptical Ghosthunter by paranormal radio talk shows on which he frequently appears ready to debunk anything from orbs to phantom voices on recorders. However, members of his team, which includes consulting mediums, are mostly staunch believers in the paranormal. Considering this strange mix of believers and skeptics, I think the Spookhunters are one of the most objective investigative groups I have been associated with. It was Owen Sliter who arranged with the National Park Service, plus a healthy fee, to allow his Spookhunter team inside the old fortress for an after-hours ghost hunt. I was invited along as the team's "consulting historian" to capture details of the investigation for publication. Little did I know at the time, it would be in this old fort where I would have a face-to-face encounter with a "ghost."

Completed in 1672, the Castillo de San Marcos, which you'll find in this guide, is the only medieval structure in the United States and apparently St. Augustine's Grand Central Station for ghosts, if we are to believe all the stories. The Spookhunters entered the Castillo after dark, accompanied by three National Park Rangers. I think the rangers were there to make sure we did not steal the cannons; other than that, the whole place was open to us. Outside the Castillo's massive stone walls, streaks of lightning pierced the darkness as a thunderstorm rumbled over the area, making it a perfect night for ghost hunting. The team immediately went about checking the dungeon-like rooms for electromagnetic anomalies while two members diligently tried conjuring up a spirit by working an Ouija Board.

After observing the investigation for about an hour, I decided to venture off on my own through a low portal, which almost required me crawling, into one of the fort's many dark rooms. The room was as black as pitch, I could not see my hand in front of my face, and emanating from the damp walls was a musty smell that took my thoughts back to time when prisoners had been confined in the place. I did not have a flashlight but did have a 35mm camera. I wondered what would happen if I took a picture in the darkness. Would I catch a ghost or some other anomaly? I raised my camera and snapped a picture. In the split second of the flash I distinctly saw a British soldier, in full-dress uniform, like straight out of 1775. He was standing not more than two feet in front of me. This is when the hair on the back of your neck stands up and wiggles. I bumped my head getting out of that place. I found a flashlight and went back into the room, where I found my "ghost" standing at attention in strict military fashion. It seems the room was used to store exhibit items and my "ghost," well, he turned out to be an exhibit mannequin dressed in a British uniform. Hey, when you're on a ghost hunt you're primed to encounter a spirit. So, let this be a lesson that every bump in the night is not necessarily a ghost.

I have been asked if I believe in ghosts. My answer is that there's no doubt weird stuff happens, as experienced by people and registered on instruments. I'm skeptical about some things and mystified by others. I have seen tables levitate and chalk mysteriously write messages during séances, but cannot say for certainty it was the work of spirits or some other unexplained force. I still consider orbs captured by digital cameras a photographic anomaly and not necessarily spirit energy. On the other hand, I believe poltergeist activity is a very real phenomenon, because the cases are well-documented and supported by testimony from multiple witnesses including professional investigators and academics. Yet, I firmly believe that eighty percent of all unexplained phenomena, whether related to hauntings, UFOs, or hairy Bigfoot creatures, can be explained as hoaxes, misinterpretations, hallucinations, or optical illusions. The remaining twenty percent is what intrigues me, because it's where we find well-documented encounters with the unknown that boggle scientific minds and scare the pants off regular folks. As previously stated, every bump in the night is not a ghost, so I'll leave it up to you to figure out how to separate the ghost bumps from plain ol' goose bumps.

Thanks to Chad Lewis and Terry Fisk you can now add *The Florida Road Guide to Haunted Locations* to your ghost buster toolbox. If you're a leader of a paranormal investigative group in Florida, this is your text book for new members. However, before you strike out in search of the unknown, let me reiterate a few words of warning passed down from my old granny: "Some things are best left alone."

Charlie Carlson
Known as Florida's Master of the Weird
and author of *Weird Florida*

ix

ACKNOWLEDGMENTS

We would like to thank Nisa Giaquinto, Sarah Szymanski, Amber Boyce-Fisk, and Jeannine Fisk for assisting us with the research and production of this book.

We are especially grateful to Tamara Gleason & Dawnette Cook, Todd Lewis, Charlie Childes, Ken Oden & Bonnie Morehardt, Cyndi Myers & Boomer, Dick Flitz & Chris Carter, Bryon & Deborah McCutchen, Pat Inmon, Stuart & Eileen Johnson, Bill Mock, Betty Davis & Big Bend Ghost Trackers, and Rita Strugala & Southern Paranormal Research Society.

We also want to thank the many people who provided us with cases, directions, and personal accounts.

INTRODUCTIONS

My first visit to Florida came in 1976 when I was only a year and a half old. My mother tells me that our family visited Disney World, but of course I have no memory of hanging out with Mickey and Minnie. Actually, I don't remember any part of that trip. However, my second visit to the Sunshine State came when I was four years old, and this time it was much more eventful. Luckily this time we avoided the ever growing pull of Disney, and instead I decided to mingle with the bizarre lizard creatures that seemed to be running around everywhere in Florida. Having been a life long Wisconsin resident, I had never seen such cool lizards living free in the wild. It felt like I had been transported to some remote island that was filled with mysterious creatures. With much effort I was finally able to capture a small lizard and I decided that I would take him home with me. I prepared a very nice box home for my new travel companion and prepared him for the journey back to the North Woods of Wisconsin.

So there I was, an innocent looking four-year-old kid, plotting to smuggle some precious cargo out of Florida back to my home in Wisconsin. Somehow I was able to sneak the creature onto the airplane without detection and I soon introduced it to the Wisconsin landscape of my backyard. Unfortunately the stress of flying, combined with the cool temperatures of Wisconsin, did not sit well with the lizard and he soon passed away. However, the abrupt end to my smuggling career taught me a thing or two about life. It showed me that the best parts of Florida did not reside inside the magical kingdom of Disney. The best parts were the wild places where people and land blended together to create a unique lifestyle and culture.

The whole fiasco also opened my eyes to the fact that Florida was a place where mystery lived, because if Florida was the home to those amazing lizards, then God only knows what else might be lurking there as well. It was with that sense of curiosity that I began my adventure into the haunted locations of the state.

Fast forward 28 years. It was the year 2007 and I was once again back in Florida doing some searching. This time I was searching for the paranormal instead of lizards. I began with a simple plan. I would start in Key West and work my way up north through the state. I started out looking for the possessed "Robert the Doll." From there I made my way north, and after scouring the state for the weird and unexplained, I found that I was slowly drifting back to myself as that wide-eyed four-year-old kid hunting for lizards. That excitement of adventure that I felt so many years ago still rang clearly in my head, and while I was trampling through the Everglades looking for the Skunk Ape, or walking the Drawdy Rouse cemetery in Orlando searching for disembodied lights, I simply let curiosity guide me along my adventure. After dozens of investigations, hundreds of witness interviews, and weeks of digging through old archives, it was time to head home. And although I did not smuggle any lizards with me this time, I once again left with the belief that mystery truly does live in Florida.

Keep an eye out,

Chad Lewis

I know that if I wasn't scared, something's wrong, because the thrill is what's scary.

—Richard Pryor

All of us want a thrill. Most tourists come to Florida for the thrill of watching a space shuttle launch or swimming with dolphins or having their picture taken with Mickey Mouse. Some of us, however, travel the state in search of a different kind of thrill—the kind that scares us. In fact, we're not just hoping for thrills, we want chills. You know, the kind of chills that go down your spine. We want the physical sensation of feeling the hair on the back of our necks standing up and goosebumps forming on our arms. This is the kind of adrenaline rush we're seeking.

In my search for thrills in Florida, I've been to Gulf Breeze looking for UFOs, and I've trudged through the swamps of Florida on Skunk Ape expeditions, but my quests were in vain. The chance of seeing the Skunk Ape is greater than one in a million; the chance of seeing a UFO is about one in a hundred; but the chance of having a ghostly experience is probably better than one in ten. At least, your odds are better when you know the right places to travel to. If you don't know where to go, it can be frustrating. You're more likely to end up on a wild-goose chase than you are to experience goosebumps. This frustration was aptly expressed in an old newspaper article with the headline of "Ghost" published in the January 4, 1872 issue of the *St. Augustine Star*:

> Somebody tried last Thursday night to get up a ghost at the fort, but it was a failure. Lots of people went there about 9 o'clock at night; we were one of them, but the ghost didn't amount to much... We don't think much of these sham ghosts. If they could get up a real bonafide ghost, such as we read about, there would be some fun in it and everybody would go and see it.

How can you avoid the "sham ghosts" and find the "real bonafide ghosts" that you read about? You can begin by using the road guide you're currently holding in your hands. If you've seen the television programs about ghosts and ghost hunters, and always wanted to be a participant rather than just a spectator, here's your opportunity. We tell you where to find some of the most haunted places in Florida. We list public places known to have a long history of haunting activity and multiple eyewitnesses. These are the locations where you have a greater chance that something unexplained just might happen.

In Florida, you can do your sightseeing in the sunlight and your thrill seeking in the moonlight. So invite a friend, grab a flashlight, and bring this book. Let the thrills begin!

Terry Fisk

CENTRAL FLORIDA

Captain & the Cowboy

Location: Apopka, Orange County, Florida
Address: 604 East Main Street, Apopka, FL 32703-5461

Ghost Lore

The Captain & the Cowboy, a popular seafood and steak restaurant, has gone out of business, as did the previous restaurant, the Townsend Plantation. Some say it's because of the economy; others say the building is cursed, as it sits on an ancient Indian burial ground; and there are even those who whisper that the place is haunted because of a tragic killing that happened there long ago.

- Near the restaurant, an apparition of a Native American hunting game has been seen crossing Orange Blossom Trail (a.k.a. Main Street or Hwy 441).

- Loud banging noises emanate from the attic. The sound of

footsteps and movement have been hear throughout the building.

- Shadowy apparitions.

- Cold spots.

- Strange lights.

- An uneasy feeling and the feeling of being watched.

- The sensation of somebody brushing against you, when nobody is there.

History

7500 BCE – This area was inhabited by Native Americans who lodged on the shores of Lake Apopka. For reasons unknown, they had disappeared by the first century CE.

1564 – French explorers discovered the Acuera Indians of the Timucua confederation living in the region.

1730 – The Acuera people were wiped out by the diseases brought by Spanish explorers.

Early 1800s – Seminoles moved into the area and named it *Ahapopka* (meaning "the potato eating place"), which is where the name of the current city was derived. It was here that the famous war chief Coacoochee ("Wild Cat") was born.

1832 – Under the terms of the Treaty of Paynes Landing, the Seminoles were supposed to migrate west of the Mississippi River, but many of them, led by chief Osceola, refused to go.

1835 to 1842 – The Second Seminole War. After seven years of bloody battle, the Seminole people surrendered.

1842 – The Armed Occupation Act forced the Seminoles to relocate to the west and opened the door for the armed occupation and settlement of the region by white settlers.

1845 – Florida became the 27th U.S. state.

1882 – The town of Apopka was incorporated.

1903 – A Queen Anne revival style house was built for the Eldredge family at 21 North Highland Avenue, near the Edgewood Cemetery. It was the first tract of land in the Apopka area purchased from the U.S. government.

1940 – The house was sold to Dr. Thomas E. McBride and his wife Helen. "Doc Tommy," as he was affectionately known, used the house as a hospital and infirmary and was the city's first practicing physician.

1954 – Helen McBride, a well-known pilot and flight instructor, shot and killed a business associate in the house.

1978 – Dr. McBride died at the age of 82 and the house sat vacant.

Early 1980s – McBride's son Robin donated the house to the city of Apopka.

1985 – Carl and Mary Townsend, along with their three children, purchased the house from the city and moved it to its present location. After being refurbished, expanded, and upgraded, it opened as the Townsend Plantation Restaurant. It was decorated with an agricultural and farming theme and was called a plantation due to the style of architecture.

1994 – The Townsend Plantation closed and sat abandoned for the next decade.

2001 – The building was used as a "haunted house" attraction for Halloween.

2004 – Don Green and Henry Gong purchased the property and began the second renovation of the house.

2005 – The house opened as The Captain and the Cowboy Steak and Seafood Grill.

2008 – The restaurant closed.

Investigation

There are several theories as to why this building might be haunted. It's believed it may have originally been built on an Indian burial ground, and that would account for the sighting of Native American spirits. Some think the spirits of the first owners of the house—the Eldredge family—might be disturbed because their home was moved from its original location. We also heard several rumors of a killing that occurred within the house, and our investigation confirmed the truth of those rumors.

On March 1, 1956, Helen McBride, a 49-year-old mother of four, was arrested and charged with first-degree murder after she shot and killed a business associate in the kitchen of her home. The victim was 33-year-old Charles Richard "Dick" Green, a disabled World War II veteran and bachelor. Green, a "close friend of the

family," enrolled in Mrs. McBride's flight school in 1946, and lived in the McBride home from 1947 to 1951.

The prosecution argued that Mrs. McBride and Green were lovers, and that McBride shot him to death in a fit of jealousy. McBride's story was that she shot him in self-defense. She said she had called Green that day about overdue payments on some jointly-owned property, but he "got nasty," came to her house, slapped her twice across the face, grabbed her by the throat, and knocked her to the floor. She ran to the kitchen and grabbed a .22 caliber pistol. Allegedly, he kept advancing toward her even after she had warned him she would shoot; consequently, she fatally shot him four times—twice in the chest and twice in the back. She claimed the gun just happened to be nearby on the kitchen table, as she was just getting ready to clean it when he arrived. During the entire altercation, her 60-year-old husband was upstairs reading in bed.

When Green's mother learned of her son's death, she called McBride a liar and described her son as a gentle man who would never harm a woman.

The case went to trial. In November of that same year, a jury acquitted Mrs. McBride, after deliberating for one hour and fifteen minutes. To this day, many doubt the innocence of Helen McBride, and some are convinced the restless spirit of Mr. Green haunts the place where he was killed.

Years later, the Townsend family acquired the house and moved it to its current location. Some people in town believe the move upset the spirits of the original owners—the Eldredge family.

After the Townsend Plantation closed and sat empty, a local radio station converted the building into a Halloween spook house, but several of the workers were convinced that the building housed more than just make-believe ghosts. On more than one night, performers walked off the job after having ghostly encounters that seemed to defy explanation. They would hear voices and footsteps, and one person felt an invisible entity brush up against them. Chairs that were set up in one location were later found rearranged in another spot.

Some of the crew were convinced that something strange was happening in the attic, which was off limits. Loud banging sounds could be heard coming from the third floor, which was off limits to everybody. Upon inspection, no explanation could be found for the sounds. Often people would drive by late at night and see a light in a third-story window. Workers reported that alarms would go off for no reason. Careful inspections of the building revealed no intruders—no *living* intruders, that is.

7

Cassadaga Hotel

Location: Cassadaga, Volusia County, Florida
Address: 355 Cassadaga Road, Cassadaga, FL 32706
Phone: (386) 228-2323
Website: www.cassadagahotel.com

Directions: Head south on Highway 4. Take exit 114. Turn left (east) on Cassadaga Road. Follow it to the end and the hotel will be on your right.

Ghost Lore

Cassadaga is one of the most famous spiritualist camps in the world, so it really comes as no surprise to hear stories of spirits roaming nearly all of the town's historic buildings. Foremost among these haunted buildings is the Cassadaga Hotel. Far from the modest dwelling of the early days, the hotel constantly updates its rooms and charm to the point where it attracts visitors from all over the world, both living and dead.

- The playful spirit of a young girl likes to pull tricks on the hotel's guests.
- The second floor is alive with the sounds of phantom voices.
- All of the spirits of the hotel are thought to be positive entities.

History

1875 – George Colby was led to the area of Cassadaga by his spirit guide.

1894 – The town of Cassadaga was incorporated.

1895 – Colby deeded the Cassadaga Spiritualist Camp Meeting Association over 35 acres of land.

1927 – The small quaint hotel was constructed. The hotel was designed in the revival style of Spanish influence. The hotel was owned by the National Spiritualist Society.

1979 – The hotel was purchased by Diana Morn. Until this time the hotel remained relatively primitive. The business was only open for six months out of the year, and many of the rooms did not include a bathroom.

Currently – The hotel and psychic center are open to the public and often hold paranormal events.

Investigation

It appears that spirits really like the open-mindedness of the Cassadaga Hotel. We spoke with the owner of the hotel who has been there for nearly 30 years. She informed us that so much paranormal activity takes place at the hotel that it is simply too hard to keep track of all of it.

The second floor of the hotel is believed to be home to the playful spirits of several young girls. Guests often report catching a glimpse of the ghostly image of a young girl skipping or running through the hallways. It is also on the second floor that other guests have heard the phantom sound of young girls giggling and laughing. The source of the mystifying giggling and laughing has never been found.

The spirit of one of these mischievous young girls seems to have a special fondness for women's makeup. Women staying at the hotel often discover that their makeup has inextricably gone missing. This is particularly true if the women happen to have long blonde hair. The theory is that the young girl is eternally searching for her lost mother, who is thought to have had long blonde hair.

Guests also hear the phantom voices of men talking upstairs. What really puzzles the witnesses is the fact that the men's style of speech and language make them sound as though they are from the early 1900s.

It should be noted that the welcoming of the hotel is not exclusively reserved for human sprits, because for years guests have reported seeing the spirit of a small dog walking on the staircase.

Numerous ghost research groups have conducted investigations at the hotel. The researchers have recorded unknown voices on their audio recorders (EVPs) and have captured a strange mist or fog-like substance on their cameras. Guests often bring cameras along with them on their visit and have captured similar phenomena as the investigators.

Island Hotel & Restaurant

Location: Cedar Key, Levy County, Florida
Physical Address: 373 Second Street, Cedar Key, FL 32625
Mailing Address: P.O. Box 460, Cedar Key, FL 32625-0460
Phone: (352) 543-5111
Toll-Free: 1-800-432-4640
Fax: (352) 543-6949
Email: info@islandhotel-cedarkey.com
Website: http://islandhotel-cedarkey.com/main.html

Ghost Lore

In 2001, there was a horror film called *Thir13en Ghosts*, which was a remake of a 1960 film of the same name.   Sometimes real-life imitates art, as in the case of the Island Hotel in Cedar Key, which is rumored to be the home of thirteen ghosts. It's a hotel that has survived hurricanes, fires, the Civil War, and Great Depression, and it houses phantom residents who have apparently survived death.

- Lights will flicker and turn off and on by themselves.

- Doors open and close or lock and unlock on their own.

- Cold spots.

- The feeling of being watched or followed.

- Room keys and other objects disappearing and reappearing in strange places.

- The piano in the lobby will play on its own.

- Numerous apparitions.

- Rooms 27, 28, and 29 are said to be haunted.

History

1859 – The property was purchased by business partners Major John D. Parsons and Francis E. Hale.

1860 – They built Parson and Hale's General Store.

1861 to 1865 – During the Civil War, Union troops invaded Cedar Key and burned down most of the buildings but spared the store and used it as a barracks and warehouse. Later it was used by Confederate troops after they retook Cedar Key.

1867 – John Muir, the famous naturalist and author, made his thousand-mile walk from Kentucky to Cedar Key and may have visited the store.

1884 – The general store also operated as a restaurant and boarding house.

1888 – Parsons died at the age of 71.

1890s – President Grover Cleveland may have stayed at the boarding house.

1896 – A hurricane destroyed much of Cedar Key. The store was damaged but intact.

1910 – Francis Hale died. Parsons' son Langdon continued to run the store.

1915 – Simon Feinberg purchased the general store and turned it into a hotel known as the Bay Hotel. It was managed by a man named Marcus Markham.

1919 – May 11. Feinberg died in the hotel under mysterious circumstances.

1930s – The hotel, then known as Fowler's Wood, was used as a brothel and speakeasy. During the depression, the bank foreclosed on the hotel and the owner may have attempted to burn it down on three different occasions, but the fire department was right across the street and managed to extinguish the fire each time.

1945 – The King Neptune Lounge was added.

1946 – Bessie and Loyal "Gibby" Gibbs purchased the rundown hotel and renovated it. It reopened as the Island Hotel and had a

great reputation. Over the years, many famous people stayed there: author Pearl Buck; singers Vaughan Monroe and Tennessee Ernie Ford; and actors Frances Langford, Myrna Loy, and Richard Boone.

1962 – Gibby died.

1973 – Bessie sold the hotel to Charles and Shirley English.

1975 – Bessie died in a tragic house fire at the age of 84.

1978 – Harold Nabors purchased the hotel.

1980 – He sold it to Marcia Rogers. The restaurant became popular after Rogers hired talented Chef Jahn McCumbers.

1980s – Singer Jimmy Buffett was a frequent guest at the hotel.

1984 – The hotel was placed on the National Register of Historic Places. Bill and MaryLou Stewart purchased the hotel.

1992 – Tom and Allison Sanders purchased the hotel.

1996 – Dawn Fisher and Tony Cousins bought the hotel from them.

2001 – Bill and MaryLou Stewart of Texas purchased the hotel.

2002 – For unknown reasons, the Stewarts fired the entire staff, boarded up the hotel, and moved back to Texas. Ownership went back to the Cousins who reopened the hotel and restaurant.

2004 – The Cousins sold the business to the current owners, Andy and Stanley Blair.

Investigation

Young Boy. When the hotel operated as Parson and Hale's General Store, a nine-year-old black boy was employed to clean up and assist around the store. One day he was wrongfully accused of stealing and chased out of the store by the manager. The young man disappeared and was never seen again. A year later, his skeletal remains were discovered in a cistern in the basement. It is believed that the scared, young man tried to hide in the tank and accidentally drowned. Many believe the ghost of the boy still hides in the basement.

Confederate Soldier. This is the most commonly seen apparition in the hotel. Early in the morning, numerous guests have seen a Confederate soldier standing at attention near the doors leading to the stairs. Could this be the original owner, Major John D. Parsons, who was a commander in the Southern army?

Simon Feinberg. When Simon Feinberg owned the hotel and restaurant, he confronted his manager, Marcus Markham, because he suspected Markham was running an illegal still on the side. After eating the evening meal that was prepared for him by Markham, Feinberg went to bed, but in the morning he was found dead in his bed. Although there was never an investigation, many

suspected Feinberg had been poisoned by Markham. Since his death, guests have seen the restless ghost of Feinberg wandering through the hotel late at night. It's also believed that he haunts room 27 where he died. On a side note, during a renovation in 1980, workers discovered the remnants of Markham's still hidden in the attic behind a fake ceiling.

Marcus Markham. Years later, Markham and a steam boat captain were drinking in the King Neptune Lounge when they got into a heated argument. A fight broke out, and Markham was stabbed to death. His ghost has been seen behind the bar near the pantry where the fatal attack occurred.

The Prostitute. It's rumored that a prostitute was murdered in one of the rooms when the hotel was used as a brothel during the Depression. She haunts rooms 27 and 28. In the middle of the night, some male guests have felt her sit on their bed and kiss them on the cheek. When the light is turned on, she quickly vanishes before their eyes.

Bessie Gibbs. This previous owner thinks she still owns the place. She likes to clean the rooms and rearrange the furniture. She's also quite the joker and enjoys locking guests out of their rooms. People have seen her wander into their rooms in the middle of the night, then vanish through a solid wall.

A séance determined the hotel was haunted by thirteen ghosts, with the spirit of Bessie Gibbs being the most dominant. Besides the six aforementioned ghosts, it's believed the hotel is haunted by a thin man, a tall man, a fisherman, and two Native Americans.

Daytona Playhouse

Location: Daytona Beach, Volusia County, Florida
Address: 100 Jessamine Boulevard,
Daytona Beach, FL 32118-3735
Phone: (386) 255-2431
Email: boxoffice@daytonaplayhouse.org or publicity@daytonaplayhouse.org
Website: www.daytonaplayhouse.org

Ghost Lore

It was a sad story. A young couple living in Daytona Beach was expecting the birth of their first child, but the husband was called off to war. Upon receiving the news of her husband's death, the young mother-to-be drowned herself in the Halifax River. Now the grieving spirits of the man and wife wander the halls of a playhouse built where their house once stood, seemingly unaware of each other's ghostly presence.

- A sense of being watched.

- People experience cold spots or get goose bumps.

- A shadowy figure in the director's booth.

- Cold spots.

- Doors opening and closing on their own.

- Strange sounds.

- Apparitions of a man and a woman wearing 1930's style clothing. They have been seen sitting in the audience, near the stage, backstage, or in the dressing room. They are always seen separately, but never together.

History

Early 1930s – Alice Beckwith and her lover, Andrés Doern, lived in a fifteen-room house on this property.

1936 to 1939 – The Spanish Civil War was fought. Doern died in battle in Spain. Alice committed suicide in the nearby Halifax River.

1946 – In December, an amateur theatre group, The Daytona Beach Little Theatre, was organized by four married couples.

1947 – In March, their first play, *Nothing, But the Truth,* was presented at the Seabreeze High School.

1948 – They set up a theatre in a former World War II WAACS barrack.

1951 – A fire destroyed the buildings, along with all their props, scripts, and costumes.

1954 – The group purchased the lot where the home of Alice Beckwith and Andrés Doern had once stood.

1955 – They built the Little Theatre, later known as the Daytona Playhouse. Their first production was *Sabrina Fair.*

1957 – The Unitarian Universalist Society occasionally used the building for religious services.

1972 – The hauntings began.

1982 – The first paranormal investigation in the playhouse took place.

Investigation

Over the years, several ghost researchers have visited the playhouse. In 1982, a team of psychics from Daytona Beach Community College toured the building. They allegedly made contact with the spirit of Alice Beckwith, described as an attractive young blond wearing a large plumed hat. They also communicated with Andrés Doern. Through their psychic channeling they learned the tragic story of the couple's demise.

When Tom Iacuzio, of the Central Florida Ghost Research organization, visited the playhouse, he was sitting in the dressing room next to a rack of clothes, when he had the unnerving experience of seeing the garments suddenly move as if an invisible hand had swept across them.

Since 1972, the theater company has had regular visitations from the forlorn ghostly couple.

Mysterious Ghost Lights

Location: Fort Meade, Polk County, Florida
Address: Keller Road, Fort Meade, FL

Directions: Take Highway 98 east out of town. Turn right on Keller Road and follow it out. Just as you pass Dishong St. (on your right) Keller Road will curve to the left. Follow the road until you get to the property gate of the Mosaic Mining Company and you will see the large hill. This is the area where the lights have been frequently spotted. However, the lights have also been seen throughout the entire area.

Ghost Lore

For centuries mysterious lights have plagued communities through-out the country. Some of the most famous cases involve the Brown Mountain Lights of North Carolina, the Paulding Light of Michigan, the Hornet Spook Light of Missouri, and the Marfa

Lights of Texas. From refracted headlights and taillights of passing cars to disembodied spirits of the deceased to earth energy to hoaxes, researchers continue to speculate and argue on the cause or origin of these lights. But while the researchers continue to try to explain the mysterious lights, the people of Fort Meade continue to observe the lights.

History

2004 – The Mosaic Company was incorporated. The company mainly mines for phosphate and is a producer of nitrogen and animal feed ingredients.

Investigation

The legends of the mysterious lights hovering around the outskirts of Fort Meade have been passed down from generation to generation. We have been able to track stories of the lights back to the 1950s and it is possible that these lights had been seen long before that.

We spoke with a woman who has lived in the community her whole life. Forty years ago the woman lived as a child out near Keller Road where she and her friends would play near where the lights were spotted. She recalls that many older kids would drive out to the area to try to catch a glimpse of the mysterious lights.

A local woman told us that when she was in high school the lights often appeared over the area. She stated that the lights would often dance around in the night sky moving in all directions.

Many skeptical residents believed that the lights were nothing more than search lights from some aircraft that could not be seen. Others believed the lights were nothing more than phosphorus from the nearby mines; however, the mines were not constructed until long after the 1950s.

Lake Helen Cemetery "Devil's Chair"

Location: Lake Helen, Volusia County, Florida
AKA: The Cassadaga Cemetery

Directions: From I-4, take exit 114 toward DeLand, and go west on State Road 472. Turn right at Dr. Martin Luther King Jr. Blvd. (W. Volusia Beltline). Turn right at Cassadaga Rd. Turn left at Matanzas St. Turn right at W. Kicklighter Rd. Turn left at Root St., and you will be at the cemetery.

Ghost Lore

You can become hot and thirsty in hell, so it's not surprising the Devil would enjoy an occasional beer. Legend has it that Lucifer has a brick throne in this cemetery, and if you leave him a can of beer as an offering, in the morning you will find an empty can.

- Shadowy figures move through the cemetery.

- Mysterious orbs of light have been seen.

- Cold spots have been felt.

- Apparitions and even Satan himself have been seen in the cemetery.

History

1872 – The Lake Helen Cemetery was established. The first to be buried was seven-year-old George E. Thatcher.

1894 – George P. Colby, a New Yorker and trance medium, founded a 55-acre spiritualist camp in Cassadaga.

1933 – Colby died on July 27th at the age of 85 and was buried in the Lake Helen Cemetery.

2008 – Lake Helen Day. A volunteer effort was organized by Janet Miller, Bill Kumbera, and Judy Hodges to clean and repair the damage to the cemetery that resulted from years of neglect and vandalism.

Investigation

Legend trippers who travel to Cassadaga and ask for directions to the Cassadaga Cemetery are usually told there is no cemetery in Cassadaga. Technically, this is true, as the cemetery is situated near the border between Cassadaga and Lake Helen, but is actually in the township of Lake Helen, despite the fact that it's closer to the town of Cassadaga. In addition, most of the people buried in the cemetery were former residents of Cassadaga. But the locals try to misdirect the curiosity seekers due to the problems they've had with vandalism in the cemetery. We do ask that you show respect for this community and for the final resting place of their friends and family.

Most people who do eventually find the cemetery become confused when they discover that it actually features three brick chairs. The one pictured above, sitting on top of a hill, is the seat considered by most to be the Devil's Chair.

People who claim to have had the experience of conversing with the Devil describe hearing a whisper in their ear or voice in their head. The discourse immediately stops when they stand up from the chair.

Some psychics claim there is a large geomagnetic vortex in this area that has attracted mediums and spiritualists to this place, but at the same time it opens the door for ghosts to readily appear.

Charlie Carlson, author of *Weird Florida,* questioned Cassadaga historian Louis Gates about the chair, and Gates gave the explanation that it was constructed by an older gentleman back in the 1920s. The man's wife had passed away suddenly, and he would visit her grave daily but had a difficult time standing, due to his arthritis. For this reason, he built the chair to have a place to sit and rest whenever he paid his respects.

The Dares. First, if you dare to sit in the Devil's Chair, Satan will appear before you and have a conversation with you. Second, if you leave an unopened can of beer at the chair, in the morning it will be either opened and empty or, in some cases, *unopened* and empty. Third, if you sit in the chair after midnight or on Halloween, some unseen force will grip you and hold you in the chair. You might be trapped there for several minutes, until it finally releases you.

Warning. Any persons caught in the cemetery after dark will be prosecuted due to the long history of vandalism and loitering.

Spook Hill

Location: Lake Wales, Polk County, Florida
Address: North Wales Drive, Lake Wales, FL 33859

Directions: Head north on Highway 17 (North Scenic Highway) and turn right onto Highway 17A. Turn right on north Wales Road, and you will see Spook Hill.

Ghost Lore

Since the time Americans fell in love with automobiles, spook hills, gravity roads, and mystery streets have become a treasured part of Americana. Generations of families have flocked to these bizarre roadside attractions hoping to discover the secret as to why their car rolls uphill while in neutral. For many, the explanation is not nearly as important as the thrill of the anomaly. From killer ghosts and phantom children, to ley lines and earth magnets, numerous solutions to the phenomenon are often proposed. For Spook Hill in

Lake Wales, the best way for you to solve the mystery is by simply visiting the place for yourself. Oh, and make sure to watch out for the giant gator.

- The protective spirit of a Native American will push your car uphill.

- The area is haunted by the vengeful spirit of an alligator.

History

The official legend states that a tribe of Seminoles who broke away from the Cherokee nation settled near the lake. For years the tribe enjoyed the fresh water and good fishing that the lake provided them. Then one day a huge alligator decided to claim the lake as his own. The alligator's presence kept the tribe in constant state of fear. Their chief, Cufcowellax, was so distraught by the fear his tribe lived under that he set out to capture the gator. Legend states that after several days he finally found the creature on the north-west shore of the lake. A terrific battle ensued and when all was said and done the chief emerged from the water victorious. Their legendary battle had created a smaller lake near the larger one. Years later, when the chief passed away, the tribe buried him on the shore of the lake in an area now considered sacred.

Source: City of Lake Wales

Investigation

The strangeness of the hill was said to be first discovered by circuit riders who delivered mail on the old trail around Lake Ticowa. The riders noticed that their horses were laboring hard while going "downhill," so they named the place "Spook Hill." Years later, local citrus growers experienced the same problem as they took the fruit to market. More recently, the road was paved and motorists discovered their automobiles also struggled while going downhill, thus adding to the reputation of Spook Hill.

It is believed that the anomaly is caused by the spirit of Chief Cufcowellax who rises from his grave to push cars uphill. Another version of the legend states that it is the angry spirit of the killed gator that continues to haunt the area and people.

We determined that Spook Hill is actually just an illusion. Even though your car appears to be rolling uphill, you are in fact moving downhill. But don't take our word for it, check it out for yourself, and be sure to pay your respects to the chief.

Seven Sisters Inn

Location: Ocala, Marion County, Florida
Address: 828 Southeast Fort King Street,
Ocala, FL 34471-2320
Phone: (352) 867-1170
Toll-Free: 1-877-888-4886
Fax: (352) 867-5266
Email: sevensistersinn@live.com
Website: www.thesevensistersinn.com
Facebook: www.facebook.com/l/398a7

Ghost Lore

Until recently, the Seven Sisters Inn consisted of two Victorian
mansions—the Scott House (pink house built in 1888) and the
Rheinauer House (purple house built in 1890). The inn has
received numerous accolades over the years, including "Inn of the
Month" by *Country Inns Bed & Breakfast Magazine* and "Best

Restoration Project" by the Florida Trust for Historic Preservation. It's listed on the National Register of Historic Places and has been highlighted in *Southern Living, Conde Naste Traveler,* and *National Geographic.* Most recently, it was featured on TV's *Ghost Hunters* and had the distinction of being declared "officially haunted."

It is said that during the Seminole Wars a battle was fought in Ocala and a triage hospital was set up on the property where the two houses currently stand. According to legend, a woman named Lizzy came to Ocala in search of her husband. She discovered he had been wounded in battle and was being treated at the military hospital. She stayed with him until he died, but remained in Ocala to help other wounded soldiers. It's believed her spirit, along with others, now inhabits the houses that were built on this ground.

- The ghost of Lizzy will tuck guests into bed and stroke their hair.

- The ghost of an older man smoking a cigar is seen sitting in a chair. Often people detect the unmistakable scent of his cigar.

- The ghost of a young boy who loves to play pranks has been encountered.

- The sound of footsteps going down the upstairs hallway.

- The sound of voices. Guests have heard a young boy calling for his mother. Others have heard the sound of a man's deep voice saying, "get out!"

- Doors open and slam on their own. The front door will open even when it's locked.

- Lights flicker and turn on and off.

- Books move or fly off the shelf.

- Shoes and other objects go missing.

- Candles won't stay lit.

- An end table keeps getting tipped over.

- People have been tripped while walking up and down the stairs, only to be pulled back and prevented from falling at the last minute.

History

Ocala, Florida

1821 – The U.S. acquired Florida from Spain.

1823 – The Treaty of Moultrie Creek forced the Seminoles onto a reservation in central Florida.

1827 – The city of Ocala did not yet exist, but Fort King was built near the corner of what would later be East Fort King Street and 39th Avenue in present-day Ocala. According to tradition, a military triage was set up where the two houses currently sit.

1835 – The Second Seminole War broke out. Resisting the move, Osceola ambushed and killed Indian agent Gen. Wiley Thompson who was in charge of persuading the Seminoles to move onto the reservation. Thompson was shot fourteen times and scalped. Four other troops were killed that same day.

1836 to 1837 – Fort King was abandoned for nearly twelve months after the Seminoles attacked it and burned it.

1842 – At the end of the Seminole War, the Indians were moved, and the fort closed.

1844 – The fort was converted into a courthouse.

1846 – Ocala became the county seat for Marion County.

1885 – Ocala was legally incorporated.

1881 – The railroad reached Ocala and the city grew as people and businesses moved in.

1883 – On Thanksgiving, a fire destroyed much of the town.

Scott House
(AKA Pink House)

1888 – During the rebuilding of the town, Gordon Sheppard Scott (1860-1943) built a three-story, Victorian-style home on Fort King Street. In August, the construction was completed, and Scott and his wife Mary Kathleen Scott (1863-1940) moved their family into the house. He was the owner of G. S. Scott & Son's Insurance and secretary/treasurer of the Ocala Building and Loan Association.

1925 – The house was converted into a duplex, but still owned by the Scott family.

1935 – Dr. & Mrs. E. Laurence Scott, Ocala's first orthopedic surgeon, turned the house to a single-family residence.

1959 – Mrs. H.C. Dozier Jr., the granddaughter of the late G.S. Scott, retained the house and returned it to a two-family dwelling.

1966 – The house was sold and converted into a tenement house known as Mrs. Riley's Boarding House. It fell into disrepair.

1982 or '83 – Mr. & Mrs. Robert C. Fair bought the house and completely restored it to its original grandeur. The first floor was occupied by the Slender Your Figure Salon owned by Mrs. Lexy Fair. The second floor was turned into a condominium for the Fair family. Mr. Fair owned and operated the Fair & Son Inc. in Ocala.

1985 – Norma Johnson and her husband purchased it and converted it into a bed and breakfast with 4-5 rooms for rent on weekends only. She named it the Seven Sisters after herself and her siblings: Norma, Lottie, Nanette, Dawn, Judy, Sylvia, and Loretta.

1989 – The bed and breakfast was acquired by pilots Bonnie Morehardt and her husband Ken Oden. When they added more guest rooms to the building, it was classified as an inn.

2008 – In February, Unexplained Research LLC conducted an investigation of the Scott House. In July, TAPS spent four days at the inn filming an investigation that aired on SyFy's *Ghost Hunters* series in early October.

2009 – In April, First Coast Community Bank foreclosed on the house. In July, the house was bought by three local attorneys: Rick Perry, Jim Richard, and Ralph Pressley. It was remodeled into a law office.

Rheinauer House
(AKA The International House, Purple House)

1890 or '91 – Joseph T. and Linda Lancaster built the house next door to the Scott House. This was the third house built on this property. The second one had burned.

1895 – Charles and Emma Rheinauer bought the house. Charles, a prominent Jewish businessman, was the director of the Merchant's National Bank and owned the Rheinauer & Brothers department store and the La Criola Cigar Manufacturing Company.

1925 – In May, Charles died after a brief illness.

1942 – Emma Rheinauer died. She was the longest inhabitant in the house.

1943 – The Rheinauer estate sold the house to Mr. & Mrs. Otto Westtstein. Over the years it had several owners: Mr. & Mr. Fred Pfeiffer, Mr. & Mrs. Joe Moses, Pat C. Reily, Mr. & Mr. Jordan West, and M.W. Reeder.

1980s – It was owned by Mr. & Mrs. Charles E. Bailey. The first floor housed the law offices of Mary Ann Huey and John Lynch. The second floor was decorated in 19th century furniture and used by the Baileys whenever they were in Ocala.

2000 – Ken Oden and Bonnie Morehardt bought the house and converted it into the International House as part of the Seven Sisters

Inn bed and breakfast.

2008 – In February, Unexplained Research LLC conducted an investigation of the International House. In July, TAPS spent four days at the inn filming an investigation that aired on SyFy's *Ghost Hunters* series in early October.

2009 – In April, First Coast Community Bank foreclosed on the house. In July, the house was bought by three local attorneys: Rick Perry, Jim Richard, and Ralph Pressley.

2010 – The house was acquired by Shiva Ramberran and Jimmy Reid along with their wives. In late April or early May of 2010, the Seven Sisters Inn reopened. Charlie Childes was the only former employee to return.

Investigation

We spoke with the former owners, Bonnie Morehardt and Ken Oden, who are both retired commercial airline pilots and friends of Ocala residents John Travolta (also a pilot) and Kelly Preston.

Morehardt and Oden told us they decorated the inn with décor collected during their world travels, including a 250-year-old doorway from a temple in Bali and hand-carved doors from Indonesia. After strange things began to happen in the house, the couple suspected they may have unwittingly brought some residual haunting energy back with these items.

The innkeeper Charlie Childes is a charming New England native who entertained us by playing the piano and sharing stories about his family history; one ancestor was persecuted during the Salem Witch Trials. Charlie said it's not the houses that are haunted, but rather the grounds on which they sit. There's a legend that both homes were built on property that was once a battlefield and triage when Fort King was in existence. He took us on a guided tour of the Seven Sisters Inn and talked about some of the ghostly activity that has been reported there over the years. Items get moved around—sometimes from one room to another. People hear voices and footsteps. They have the feeling of an unseen presence or experience the sense of being watched. One guest took a picture of the outside of the Rheinauerr House which showed some type of huge swirling vortex over the roof. The next day a loud flock of crows was seen flying in a circular vortex over the house in the exact same position. The owners, employers, and guests have also seen full-bodied apparitions of a woman, a young boy, and an old man.

The Woman. Years ago, when the inn operated as a boarding house, there was an elderly lady who died in what was later known as Sylvia's Room, and some believe the woman haunts it. She's described as a tall lady who wears a white dress and walks through walls—even the bathroom walls! Charlie says one guest saw her enter through the doorway, pick up a ginger jar, and drop it on the floor. The moment it shattered, she disappeared. Apparently she doesn't like it when people move things around in her room. Another guest staying in the room was looking for some reading material and took a book off the mantle. Later they returned the book, but not in the same place. They were startled to see the book move across the shelf back to its original position. This same ghostly woman has also been seen sitting in a chair reading a newspaper. She wears a big hat and according to Charlie she's dressed like "she just stepped off the Titanic." It's believed this ghost doesn't like fire. Whenever somebody lights the candles in the room, she blows them out. When Charlie attempted to light incense, he physically felt the firm grip of an invisible hand on his elbow and the sound of moaning; he decided not to light it. A couple was holding their wedding in the front parlor when they made three unsuccessful attempts to light the candles. On the third try the candles went out and flew across the room. The couple decided to proceed without candles. While researching the history of the house, it was discovered there had been a fire at one time.

The Boy. A phantom boy has been seen on the property. Somebody saw Charlie walking across the parking lot and noticed a small boy following close behind him, but the child wasn't visible to Charlie. Another time Charlie saw a pair of children's shoes sitting neatly at the top of the stairs. When he bent down to inspect them, a young boy dressed in white suddenly poked his face around the corner, then vanished. It's believed he's a mischievous little rascal who likes to hide objects and play pranks. People have been tripped while walking up and down the stairs, only to be pulled back and prevented from falling; some think the boy might be responsible. One of the housekeepers was walking down the steps when she slipped and started to fall. She felt someone grab her by the back of her shirt, pull her up the stairs, and sit her down on the top step. She thanked the ghost for saving her life. Charlie had a similar experience. Something invisible tripped him on the stairs, and he fell headlong toward a huge stained-glass window. While in mid-fall, he felt two unseen hands grab him and divert him away from the window, but then he was falling towards a coffee table. At the last minute, the hands stopped his fall and stood him upright on the floor.

The Man. In the room formerly known as the Paris Room, people have seen a man wearing a broad hat sitting in a chair smoking a cigar. After he vanishes, the scent of the cigar smoke still lingers. One of the housekeepers came face-to-face with him, but before he vanished into thin air, he picked up the chair he was sitting in and threw it over her head. Charlie has seen a man "dressed like

Abraham Lincoln" who walks through walls.

Unexplained Research LLC. We brought in the "Psychic Medium Sisters," Tamara Gleason and Dawnette Cook, to assist in our investigation. These talented sisters have worked with famed medium Allison DuBois, and they never fail to impress people with their amazing accuracy. Precautions were taken to ensure they had no advance knowledge of the inn's history or haunting activity. Upon entering the Scott House, they immediately sensed a man sitting in a chair smoking a cigar. Later they remarked that Nanette's Room was at one time a den, and they could sense bourbon and cigar smoke. When they walked into the front parlor, they picked up on the presence of a playful little boy on the staircase. In one of the rooms they also detected the presence of the woman in white. They could see her sitting in front of a mirror brushing her hair. Loretta's Room, located in the back corner of the second floor, gave them an uneasy feeling, as they sensed drugs and prostitution. In the '60s and '70s, the building operated as Mrs. Riley's Boarding House, a disreputable tenement house in neglected condition. It offered inexpensive housing for Central Florida Community College students, and this was during the height of the drug counterculture. While descending the back staircase in the Rheinauer House, the mediums experienced a sharp, stabbing pain in their abdomen, which validated the identical sensation Charlie has had previously in the same location. They believe a stabbing occurred there many years ago, but we were unable to find documentation to confirm this.

Ghost Hunters. A few months after we were there, the inn was visited by TAPS (The Atlantic Paranormal Society) of television's *Ghost Hunters*. Jason Hawes and Grant Wilson had heard the stories of people being tripped on the stairs, so Jason decided to test the claim. He removed his flip-flops and left them at the bottom of the staircase in the front parlor, so he could be certain he wasn't tripping on them. When he got to the top of the stairs, he saw a small shadowy figure dart from one room to another. It was about the size of a seven or eight-year-old child. This was the same location where Charlie had seen the boy. Jason was not tripped while walking down the stairs, but once he got to the bottom, he noticed one of his flip-flops was missing. After searching the entire house for nearly half an hour, the team eventually found it in the last room they checked. It was behind a closed door sitting in the middle of the floor in a room that Charlie hadn't even shown them on the tour. Could this be a prank perpetrated by the little boy the two mediums saw by the staircase?

In the Rheinauer House, Jason was walking past the India Room when he saw a big shadow move inside. When the two men entered to investigate, Grant noticed his K2 meter had high spikes around a chair, and he could trace the outline of a seated figure. Outside that area there was nothing. Both men sat in the chair and noticed it was about 10-15 degrees colder than the rest of the room. Twice when they rapped "shave and a haircut" on wood, they heard the "two bits" response come from somewhere else in the house. The two ghost hunters determined the house had "a steady trickling of activity that was impressive."

Foreclosure. Bonnie Morehardt and Ken Oden decided to sell the inn so they could focus on their careers. A couple of times they were ready to close a deal when misfortune intervened. One inter-

ested buyer passed away before a deal could be finalized. Later a real estate agent died while working on another potential sale. In January of 2008, a contract that would have required a potential buyer to start making mortgage payments failed. When First Coast Community Bank asked the owners for the total amount due, which they couldn't pay, the inn went into foreclosure.

Local ghost investigators and employees of the inn reported an increase in haunting activities in the inn during the weeks leading up to the foreclosure auction. On one occasion, a book flew off a shelf and shot across the room. Apparently the spirits were not happy about the change that was about to happen.

On April 7, 2009, First Coast Community Bank put the inn on the auction block and bought it from itself for $100,000. The actual value of the property exceeded $1.3 million. The sale included both Victorian houses along with all furnishings and fixtures. While the inn sat empty, the haunting activity continued. People saw shadowy figures looking out of the windows. It was also reported that the interior lights would mysteriously turn on and off.

On July 21, 2009, there was an online foreclosure auction, and a group of three local attorneys—Rick Perry, Jim Richard, and Ralph Pressley—were the winning bidders. They purchased the Scott House for $213,500 and the Rheinauer House for $258,530. Perry and Richard bought out Pressley shortly after the auction, and converted the Scott House in their law office. Two ghost hunters from Paranormal Seekers LLC, Shiva Ramberran and Jimmy Reid along with their wives, purchased the Rheinauer House in 2010. They redecorated the house and furnished it to look as it did in the 1890s. In late April or early May of 2010, the Seven Sisters Inn bed and breakfast reopened. Charlie Childes was rehired was the innkeeper. Previous owners Ken Oden and Bonnie Morehardt still live in the cottage behind the inn.

Note: The Scott House is currently a law office and no longer part of The Seven Sisters Inn. If you are hoping to have a haunting experience, we encourage you to make a reservation at the Seven Sisters Inn bed and breakfast.

Ma Barker's House

Location: Ocklawaha, Marion County, Florida
Address: East Highway 25, Ocklawaha, FL 32179

Directions: In Ocklawaha head west on E Highway 25 through downtown. The death house will be on your left and it is the second driveway before you come to the Lake Weir Laundromat. The driveway leads to two homes and it is the home on the left. If you go to the Laundromat you have gone too far.

Warning: The house is on private property so please view only from the road. **DO NOT TRESPASS!**

Ghost Lore

Nestled in their hideout house Ma Barker and her son Fred were looking for some rest and relaxation in the Florida sunshine.

Agents got word of where the two were hiding out and quickly descended on the rural small town. Agents then surrounded the lakeside house and knocked on the door and told Ma Barker that the agents were there to arrest the family. Ma said, "Let's see what Fred has to say about that," as Fred fired his machine gun out the window. An all out gun fight erupted, causing the death of both Fred and Ma. Soon after her death, Ma Barker's spirit started appearing in the windows.

History

1873 – Arizona Donnie Clark (Ma Barker) was born in Missouri.

1892 – Arizona Clark married George Barker.

1915 – The Barker boys started their life of crime.

1935 – The FBI raided the house of Ma Barker and her son Fred. After several hours of gun fighting, Ma and Fred were found dead inside the house. Ma's body had four bullets in it while Fred was filled with 11 bullets.

Currently – The home is privately owned.

Investigation

On January 16th, after a long crime spree spanning many years, Ma Barker and her son Fred were hiding out in their Lake Weir rental house when fifteen agents surrounded the place. The agents shouted out for the Barkers to surrender, and according to the *Key West Citizen*, the agents were answered with "a blaze of machine gun fire." A fierce gun battle ensued when the agents riddled the home with thousands of bullets. Shortly after the initial gunfire, the house fell eerily silent. Convinced that the Barker's were setting a trap the agents waited for any sign of life. Fred and his mother were dead, but the authorities did not know this yet, so every time the curtain blew in the wind the agents opened fired on the house. Finally, after six hours, the cautious agents sent the Barker's hired cook to check out the situation in the house. The cook discovered the dead bodies of Fred and Ma.

Most crime scholars agree that Ma Barker was certainly not the brains behind the Barker crime operation. It is much more likely that Ma was aware of her sons' criminal activities, but had no direct hand in orchestrating or committing the actual crimes.

Soon after her death, residents started seeing the ghostly image of Ma Barker peering out the windows of the home as though she was on constant lookout for the authorities.

Jerome Pohlen, in his book *Oddball Florida,* wrote that Ma Barker's ghost is often seen inside the house running a comb through her hair.

When you are done checking out Ma Barker's death house make sure you visit Ma Barker's Hideaway (13575 East Highway 25 in Ocklawaha). Inside you will find the walls covered with newspaper accounts of the shootout and a staff that is more than willing to share stories from the town's infamous past.

The Dare. If you watch the house you will see Ma Barker roaming the property.

Drawdy-Rouse Cemetery

Location: Orlando, Orange County, Florida
Address: No Address—Really, they do not have an address.
Rouse Road, Orlando, FL

Directions: Take Rouse Road from the University. The cemetery will be on the left side on Rouse Road, a half mile from the University.

Ghost Lore

During the 1840s Benjamin Miles was a hard-working local resident who died unexpectedly. His family had no means to pay for funeral so they dumped his lifeless body in an unmarked grave inside the cemetery. Each night his restless spirit rises from the grave angered by the fact that he never received a proper burial.

- Visitors who enter the cemetery are greeted by a mysterious owl that terrifies them with a high-pitched screech.

- Many unmarked graves are located all over the cemetery.

History

1871 – The Drawdy and Rouse families recognized the need for a local cemetery. Each family donated five acres of their land so that the community would have a cemetery.

1918 – During the flu epidemic that struck the area, numerous unknown bodies were buried somewhere inside the cemetery.

Currently – The cemetery is privately owned and operated by a board of trustees.

Investigation

The Drawdy–Rouse Cemetery is a closed cemetery. It contains the remains of Drawdy and Rouse family members. This means that in order for you to obtain a plot at the cemetery you must be a descendant of someone who is already buried inside the cemetery. However, throughout the years, in order to raise needed funds, a small number of non-related persons have been allowed burial inside the gates.

The legend states that the ghost of Benjamin Miles appears nightly in the cemetery and that his spirit is summoned there by the high-pitched screech of a cemetery owl. Those who have seen the ghost of Mr. Miles describe him as wearing brown or tan colored work clothes. He is believed to be a man that was buried in an unmarked grave in the cemetery during the 1840s. If Mr. Miles did indeed die in the 1840s, his grave would have been unmarked, as the cemetery was not created until 1871. It is more likely that Mr. Miles was one of the many unknown bodies buried in the cemetery in 1918 (see below). Local historians have been unable to find any record of a Benjamin Miles and his surname is not known in the area.

In 1918, a flu epidemic spread throughout the planet taking somewhere between 50-100 million lives. In Orlando many families lost their loved ones. During this time of economic hardship many people could not afford a proper burial and simply snuck into the cemetery at night and discretely buried their loved ones in unmarked graves.

The cemetery caretakers do not know the exact number of unknown bodies that were buried in the cemetery, nor do they have a record of as to where the bodies are buried. It is generally believed that the unmarked graves are located in the middle of the cemetery grounds. It is based on this assumption that the cemetery does not allow any new burials in the middle of the cemetery.

We spoke with many paranormal groups that believed the cemetery was a wicked and evil place filled with many angry spirits.

Others believe that the cemetery is plagued by mysterious cold spots that will appear even during the sweltering heat of summer. It is said that if you are overcome with a cold chill while in the cemetery it means that a spirit is nearby.

The Dare. If you listen for the screech of an owl a spirit will soon appear.

Greenwood Cemetery

Location: Orlando, Orange County, Florida
Address: 1603 Greenwood Street, Orlando, FL 32801-4112
Phone: (407) 246-2616
Website: www.cityoforlando.net/greenwood/index.htm

Directions: From Highway 408 (East-West Expy.) heading east turn right on the S. Mills Ave. exit. Turn left on Greenwood Street and the cemetery will be straight ahead.

Ghost Lore

Greenwood Cemetery is an 82-acre cemetery that is filled with plenty of rolling hills, blooming azalea shrubs, majestic trees, and of course, graves. The cemetery feels so secluded that it is hard to believe that is sits right next to the fast-paced hustle and bustle of downtown Orlando. Some of Orlando's most important pioneers rest under the shadow of the cemetery's trees. However, Orlando's oldest cemetery also casts a dark shadow of hauntings and mysterious paranormal activity.

- Unknown lights and orbs float throughout the cemetery.

- At night, spectral figures rise from the graves and wander around the cemetery.

History

1875 – The town of Orlando was incorporated.

1880 – Residents spoke out about the need for a proper cemetery in Orlando.

1880 – John W. Anderson sold twenty-six acres of land to be used as a city cemetery. The cost of the cemetery was $800.

1911 – The cemetery added an additional 40 acres that were previously owned by the city.

Source: Greenwood Cemetery

Investigation

Several different walking tours of the cemetery are available. During these tours, visitors often report seeing the ghostly image of an unknown person walking around the cemetery in the distance. Unfortunately, the wandering "person" always disappears before people can get close enough to identify the figure. Many tour-goers are surprised to find that the photos they took of various tombstones contain many floating orbs.

A reporter for the *Orlando Sentinel* took a tour of the cemetery and reported to have captured some strange orbs and other distorted photos. However, the paper's photo editor dismissed the orb photos as being nothing more than dust on the negative while the other odd photos were attributed to the poor quality of the disposable camera.

49

We spoke with several staff who told us that often while they are in the cemetery after dark they will hear odd noises. However, the staff was quick to explain these unidentified noises as nothing more than other people inside the cemetery.

One of the stories we were told about the cemetery was that the spirits of Orlando's first white pioneers are rising up from their eternal sleep to keep a close eye on how Orlando and its people are doing.

Ashley's Cafe & Lounge

Location: Rockledge, Brevard County, Florida
Address: 1609 US Highway 1, Rockledge, FL 32955-2817
Phone: (321) 636-6430

Directions: Head north on Highway 1 (Indian River Lagoon Scenic Highway) to Rockledge. The restaurant will be on your left-hand side.

Ghost Lore

Back in the 1920s, a young woman was involved in a heated argument with her boyfriend. As the argument progressed, the boyfriend became enraged, and in a fit of anger he threw his girlfriend into the storage room where he murdered her. When the woman did not return home, her family began to worry. Three days later her mutilated body was discovered along the river. Her murderer was never found, and her restless spirit continues to haunt the last place she ever saw.

51

- Much of the activity in the restaurant takes place in the women's restroom.

- The apparition of a young woman dressed in clothing from the early 1900s is spotted throughout the restaurant.

- The restaurant's alarm system will often be triggered by apparitions.

History

1933 – On New Year's Eve, Jack's Tavern opened as a liquor bar. This marked the end of prohibition, and the saloon was the first one opened in the vicinity.

1934 – The body of 19-year-old Ethel Allen was found along the riverbanks. Her body was mutilated and the victim was identified only by a tattoo that she had on her thigh.

1930s to 1980s – The restaurant and saloon went though numerous owners and names. Throughout the years, the place was called Gentleman Jim's, Sparrow Hawk, Loose Goose, and other names.

1985 – The establishment was purchased by Greg and Sue Parker.

Investigation

The young woman was not murdered in the 1920s, as most versions of the legend contend. It was actually in 1934 that Ethel Allen's body was found near the Indian River. The body was severely mutilated and was only identified by a tattoo the young lady had on her leg.

The case was never solved, making it very difficult to determine where the murder took place, but local speculation of the time pointed to the restaurant.

Many of the paranormal reports come from the storage room where the young woman was said to have met her fate. Years ago, while undergoing renovation, the storage room was converted into the women's restroom.

Many guests report going into the bathroom only to witness the toilet paper rolls dispensing on their own. Other women report seeing the water faucets turn on and off by some unseen force. Some bathroom reports are even more sinister, as several women have rushed out of the restroom complaining of an overwhelming sensation of being chocked.

Several staff told us that many nights, while they are working, plates, glasses, and bottles will often fall and break as though thrown by some unseen person.

Many guests are amazed to see the ghostly image of a young woman who is dressed as though she lived during the early 1900s.

Researcher Arthur Myers wrote in his book, *The Ghostly Register,* that visiting psychics often pick up negative energy from various past events that have taken place in the bar.

We spoke with the Rockledge Police Records Department which confirmed that the police have responded to numerous alarms at the restaurant. When the police arrived at the building no intruders were ever found.

When you visit the restaurant, make sure you check out the wall near the men's room where the restaurant has hung numerous ghostly photos taken by guests and investigators over the years.

NORTHEAST FLORIDA

Bosque Bello Cemetery

Location: Fernandina Beach, Amelia Island, Nassau County, Florida

Directions: Travel one mile north of Atlantic Avenue on North 14th Street within the city of Fernandina Beach.

Ghost Lore

Bosque Bello is Spanish for "beautiful forest," which is an appropriate name considering how beautifully forested the cemetery is with its live oak and Spanish moss. But the beauty and tranquility changes after dark when the graveyard suddenly takes on a menacing appearance. Shadows will begin to move in on you and make your blood run cold.

- The spirits of three children haunt the cemetery.

- Orbs and other anomalies appear in photos.

- Moving shadows.

- Voices and strange sounds.

- The back left corner of the cemetery is the oldest and has the most haunting activity.

History

1798 – The cemetery was established.

1945 – A new section was added to the cemetery on land donated by J. G. Cooper and Sadie Cooper.

1987 – The General Duncan Lamont Clinch Historical Society of Amelia Island surveyed the original section.

1997 – The Amelia Island Genealogy Society updated the original survey by including more recent and they also surveyed the new section of the cemetery. At that time, the cemetery contained approximately 2,000 graves.

Investigation

Several people have seen the ghosts of three children playing in the cemetery. According to Cyndi Myers, who does the ghost tours for Amelia Island Carriages, the phantom youths are usually seen frolicking near a family plot for two parents and their three young offspring.

A couple showed Myers a photo they had taken in the cemetery one night. While sitting in their car, they heard a loud thump on the back window. When they turned around, they saw two glowing eyes directly behind them. They believed it was some kind of ghostly entity because it was too tall to be a deer or any other forest creature. Quickly they grabbed their camera and snapped a picture of it. To this day the picture remains unexplained.

Florida House Inn Bed & Breakfast

Location: Fernandina Beach, Amelia Island, Nassau County, Florida
Address: 22 South Third Street,
Fernandina Beach, FL 32034-4207
Phone: (904) 261-3300
Toll-Free: 1-800-258-3301
Email: innkeepers@floridahouseinn.com
Website: www.floridahouseinn.com

Ghost Lore

Although it now sits closed, after 152 years of business, the Florida House Inn was the state's oldest surviving hotel. During its distinguished history, its guests included political leaders such as Ulysses S. Grant and Cuban revolutionary José Martí; wealthy businessmen such as the Rockefellers, Carnegies, and Henry Ford; and even Hollywood celebrities such as Mary Pickford, Stan Laurel, and

Oliver Hardy. Despite the fact the doors are no longer open for business and the rooms sit empty, some spectral guests have apparently remained behind.

- Apparitions of a young boy, a soldier, a housekeeper, and a prostitute have been reported.

- The sound of children running up and down the staircase.

- Bartenders and patrons have heard the sound of footsteps in the upstairs hallway when nobody was there.

- A pair of glowing red eyes has been seen in the kitchen and in the window.

- Doors will open and close or lock and unlock on their own.

- Windows open on their own.

- The faucet in the kitchen will turn on and off by itself.

- A toilet seat was ripped from a toilet and hurled.

- Beds shake.

- The owners have seen plates and bowls fly off the shelves in the kitchen.

- In the morning, guests have found their belongings thrown on the floor.

- A broom started to fall over, stopped midway, then righted itself.

- A lamp lights up...while unplugged.

History

1857 – It was built by David Levy Yulee (1810-1886).

1861 to 1865 – During the Civil War, Amelia Island was seized by the North, and the inn was used to house Union officers.

1865 – It was purchased by Major Thomas Leddy and his wife Annie. They built living quarters for themselves and added a dining room for guests.

1872 – Major Leddy died and Annie continued to run the business as an inn and restaurant. The inn could accommodate 35 guests. Rates were $2 per day or $3 to 10.50 per week, depending on the rooms.

1882 – An addition was built on by Mrs. Joseph Higgins.

1880s – Former US President Ulysses S. Grant stayed at the inn and gave a speech from the balcony.

1895 – Cuban revolutionary José Martí was a guest.

1930s – The inn became a saloon hotel and brothel.

1939 to 1945 – During WWII, it became a boarding house.

1990 – It was completely renovated.

1991 – Another wing was added to the back of the building.

1994 – Sammy Sailor bought the inn.

2003 – The inn was purchased by Joe and Diane Warwick.

1999 – The inn was featured on the Travel Channel's *Romantic Inns of America,* hosted by Judith Moen.

2008 – The Southern Paranormal Research Society conducted an investigation at the inn.

2010 – The inn closed after 152 years of continuously being in business.

Investigation

This clapboard Victorian building was constructed in 1857 by David Yulee's Florida Railroad. The railroad linked two major ports, one on the Atlantic Coast (Fernandina Beach) and the other on the Gulf Coast (Cedar Key). Important people from the railroad stayed at the inn. During the Civil War it housed Union officers. Over the years, a number of famous politicians, businessmen, and movie stars have slept here. Not surprisingly, the Florida House Inn is listed on the National Register of Historic Places.

The Prostitute. Historians say the inn operated as a brothel during the 1930s. Room 12 is believed to be haunted by either a prostitute or madam who was murdered there. She has been known to climb into bed with male guests who stay in the room but has an aversion to other woman. People describe her as looking dapper and apparently she likes to keep her room tidy and has been known to pick up after guests who are too sloppy.

The Widower. Several people have seen a tall man with a sullen expression wandering the hallways apparently in search of his young wife who died during childbirth at the inn. He has also been seen in other parts of the inn, and one guest claims she spoke with him for over an hour in her room. She insisted he's not a malicious spirit; he's just depressed and grieving over the loss of his beloved.

The Soldier and the Boy. In Room 1, apparitions of a Union Soldier and a young boy have been seen. The man is described as having long brown hair and wearing a military jacket. The boy, believed to have been his son, has also been seen in other parts of the inn.

The Housekeeper. Staff and guests have seen a phantom housekeeper who vanishes before their eyes. She's been spotted walking in the hallway or cleaning the rooms. It's believed she was a former employee who is long since deceased, but still enjoys working at the inn.

Southern Paranormal Research Society. In 2008, the Southern Paranormal Research Society, based in Kingsland, Georgia, brought their team to the Florida House. Ryan Smith, a reporter from the *News-Leader,* was assigned the "paranormal beat" and accompanied the team to document their investigation. As the SPRS team, led by Rita Strugala, went through the building, one of the first things to happen was a door slamming shut on its own when nobody was near it. In one of the rooms, the investigators were using digital laser thermometers and recorded a temperature drop of 27 degrees in about 20 minutes. There were no drafts or open windows, and the air conditioner was off. In a normal situation, the body heat from a group of people would have raised the temperature of a room. In Room 1, where the Union soldier and the boy have been seen, Smith described an interesting experience the team had when they noticed a curious clicking sound.

> I realize it's the third time I've heard the sound. I can even source it: it's coming from the washstand, less than 10 feet from where I'm sitting. Boehnke [a SPRS technician] has heard it too.

He flicks on his flashlight and says, "Over there. Sounds like someone's flicking paper or something." He's nearly right. There's a cellophane soap wrapper lying on the washstand. He notes the information for the benefit of the tape and turns the light off." "Can you make a noise for us?" Strugala asks. Click. "Is that you?" Click. "Is there anything we can do for you?" Silence. "Do you want us to leave?" Strugala asks. Click. That's good enough for me, by gum. Strugala and Boehnke too—they always respect a request to leave, Strugala says. Before we go, however, I just have to try something. I want to hear the sound I make when I flick that cellophane wrapper. Click. No doubt about it—the sound we heard, apparently in direct response to questions, was identical to the sound I just made by flicking that cellophane wrapper. ("A bump in the night, is it paranormal...?" by Ryan Smith, *News-Leader*.)

The SPRS was not disappointed that night. They captured a number of EVPs, including one that said, "Take a picture of the corpse," which was recorded in the room where the prostitute was allegedly murdered. A photo of the exterior of the building showed what appeared to be glowing red eyes peering from a window on the upper floor. Later, one of the investigators saw a pair of red eyes in the kitchen. After entering one of the rooms, the team noticed every battery-powered device had simultaneously stopped working, which frequently happens in haunted locations.

One of the strangest phenomena at the inn involved a lamp that sat in a small alcove in the downstairs hallway. Owner Diane Warwick explained to the team how the lamp was turned on and worked just fine for well over a year, until an employee noticed it wasn't plugged in! In fact, there wasn't even an outlet anywhere near it. They moved the lamp to a different location at the inn and plugged it in, but it never worked again. When she retrieved the lamp to demonstrate that it wasn't functional, to her surprise, it lit right up.

A special thanks to Rita Strugala and the Southern Paranormal Research Society for the information they shared.

Fort Clinch

Location: Fernandina Beach, Amelia Island, Nassau County, Florida
Address: Fort Clinch State Park, 2601 Atlantic Avenue, Fernandina Beach, FL 32034-2203
Phone: (904) 277-7274
Website: www.floridastateparks.org/fortclinch

Ghost Lore

Most of the haunted locations we investigate have a history of tragedy and death. Although Fort Clinch was used as a military base during Civil War and Spanish-American War, it never saw a battle, and there were no recorded military casualties, yet several ghosts reside within its walls.

- It's said to be haunted by the ghost of a Union soldier who broke a promise to his wife.

65

- Ghosts of Yankee soldiers have been seen standing in the courtyard.

- The infirmary is said to be haunted by a woman dressed in a white nurse's outfit carrying a lantern.

- A different woman in a white dress has been seen searching for her baby. She vanishes when approached.

- The cries of a baby are often heard.

- People have reported the sounds of footsteps (clopping boots), whispers, and the rattling of keys on a key chain.

- Orbs and other anomalies have appeared in photos.

History

1847 – Construction began on Fort Clinch, but due to a lack of government funding, it was never completed. The fort was named for General Douglas Lamont Clinch.

1861 – The Civil War began. Confederate troops used the fort.

1862 – Union troops took over the fort after General Robert E. Lee ordered a withdrawal. They used it as a base of operations until the end of the war.

1869 – The fort was placed on caretaker status.

1898 – During the Spanish-American War, troops were stationed at the fort, but after the war it was abandoned when it was determined that the fort was no longer needed.

1936 – The Civilian Conservation Corps (CCC) began restoration of the fort.

1935 – The state of Florida purchased the fort and 256 acres of land that surrounded it.

1938 – It became the Fort Clinch State Park and opened to the public.

1939 to 1945 – During World War II, the fort was closed to the public and served as a communications and security post for the Navy, Coast Guard, and Army.

1972 – The fort was added to the National Register of Historic Places.

Present – The fort remains open to the public as a historic state park.

Investigation

The Soldier in the Window. A family was touring the fort one evening, and their son wandered off on his own to do some exploring. The sky was moonless, and in the darkness the boy was startled when he heard a noise. He turned and his eye caught sight of a Union soldier standing in the third window from the left in one of the barracks. The figure seemed bright, as if illuminated from within the room. The specter made eye contact with the young boy, tipped his hat, and then vanished. At that moment the room became dark. The boy related the sighting to his parents. When they asked one of the re-enactors about it were told that several other tourists had also witnessed the apparition in the same window.

The Baby. The ghostly sounds of a crying baby and the apparition of a woman in white searching for the baby usually occur in the southwest tunnel. When the fort fell into disuse, it was common for derelicts to take shelter there. Rumor has it that in the 1920s a young homeless mother and her infant daughter were living in the fort when the baby took ill and died.

The Nurse. People have seen a phantom woman wearing a white nurse's uniform near the building that was used as the fort hospital. One night a volunteer decided to campout on the top floor. In the darkness she was fumbling through her overnight bag when sud-

67

denly a woman in white came to her assistance with the light of a lantern. The volunteer found what she was searching for and thanked the woman, whom she assumed to be another volunteer. The woman with the lantern left the room and disappeared. After carefully searching the grounds, the volunteer was unable to find the woman.

The Broken Promise. During the Civil War, a Union soldier stationed at the fort wrote his beloved wife a letter promising her he would return home alive. Sadly, he died of natural causes before seeing her. Several of the tour guides and re-enactors have seen his spirit walking in the courtyard. Apparently he's unaware that the war is over and he's fulfilled his military duty. Somewhere in the afterlife, his wife probably still awaits his return.

The Marching Soldiers. One of the most talked about experiences that happened at the fort is when some volunteers were camping there during a weekend in July. On the night of a full moon, they were sitting on a porch when their disbelieving eyes saw four phantom soldiers dressed in Confederate uniforms come marching across the grounds, up the ramp, and to the other side of the wall. A quick search failed to find the soldiers. Being intrigued, the volunteers returned a year later, in July, during the full moon, hoping to see a repeat of this ghostly spectacle. They were not disappointed. Again, the soldiers appeared after dark. As they marched across the grounds and up the ramp, one of the volunteers noticed there were only three soldiers this time, so he shouted, "Hey, where's the fourth guy!" Whereupon, one of the soldiers replied, "He's sick tonight. Couldn't come!"

The Dare. If you visit the fort in July during a full moon, phantom soldiers will appear.

The Old Jail

Location:** Fernandina Beach, Amelia Island, Nassau County, Florida
Address: The Amelia Island Museum of History (located inside the old Nassau County Jail), 233 South Third Street, Fernandina Beach, FL 32034-4210
Phone: (904) 261-7378
Fax: (904) 261-9701
Email: info@ameliamuseum.org
Website: www.ameliamuseum.org

Ghost Lore

Amelia Island, known as the "Isle of Eight Flags," has served under the flags of eight conquerors. One of those conquerors was the French-born pirate Luis Aury. When he was expelled by US forces, he left behind an illegitimate son, Luc Simon Aury, who also became a pirate and terrorized the island community. It's rumored that in the years since his bloody execution, the ghost of this notorious scoundrel still haunts the Old Jail.

- Moaning sounds.

- Voices have been heard in the building late at night.

- Apparitions of Luc Simone Aury, with a gaping slash across his throat.

History

1783 – Spain gained control of Amelia Island from the British.

1788 – Luis-Michel Aury was born in Paris, France.

1817 – June 29. Scottish-born General Gregor MacGregor and 55 men captured Fernandina from the Spanish.

1817 – September 4. A lack of funds forced Mac Gregor to turn over authority to Jared Irwin and Ruggles Hubbard.

1817 – September 13. The Battle of Amelia. Irwin and Hubbard were victorious when the Spaniards launched a counterattack.

1817 – September 17. Luis Aury sailed into the port with $60,000. Irwin and Hubbard begged for his financial assistance, which Aury granted, and in exchange he became the commander-in-chief of military and naval forces.

1817 – September 21. Aury issued a proclamation that Amelia Island was annexed to the Mexican Republic.

1817 – November 5. Hubbard died and Aury declared himself the supreme civil and military authority and imposed martial law on Amelia Island for ten days.

1817 – December 23. Aury surrendered to US forces led by Captain J. D. Henley and Jamor James Bankhead.

1818 – February. Aury left Amelia Island. According to legend, later that year, his illegitimate son, Luc Simone Aury, was born in Fernandina.

1821 – August 30. Luis Aury died on Providencia Island when he was thrown from his horse.

1830s – According to legend, Luc Simone Aury was convicted of murder, rape, robbery, and other crimes and hanged at Fernandina.

1854 – David Yulee relocated Fernandina from Old Town to its present-day location.

1878 – The Nassau County Jail was built.

1935 – A bigger county jail was built to replace the old one.

1975 – The Duncan Lamont Clinch Historical Society formed a committee to develop a museum for Amelia Island. Fernandina resident William Decker had amassed a collection of thousands of books, documents, and artifacts relating to local history.

1977 – A board of fifteen trustees from that committee incorporated themselves as a non-profit cultural institution under the name of the "Fernandina Historical Museum." The city of Fernandina Beach purchased the Decker collection and donated it to the museum.

1978 – The museum was housed in the old train depot.

1979 – After the new jail was built, the old Nassau County jailhouse sat empty and in disrepair. The museum rented the old jail and the County Commission leased it to them for $1 per year.

1980s – The County Commission donated the old jail to the museum. After having gone through several name changes, it was officially named, "The Amelia Island Museum of History."

2003 – The museum was renovated at a cost of half a million dollars.

2009 – The Jacksonville Paranormal Society conducted an investigation in the museum.

Investigation

During the latter part of 1817, Fernandina was ruled by 29-year-old Luis-Michel Aury who claimed Amelia Island for Mexico. In December of that year he surrendered to US forces, and a couple months later he fled the island . . . but not before fathering an illegitimate child—Luc Simone Aury.

The legend is widely circulated and has been passed down for several generations. As the story goes, Luc Simone Aury grew up to be an outlaw. Authorities eventually captured him, and he was convicted of murder, rape, robbery, and a long list of other heinous crimes. When the young man was sentenced to die by hanging, word of the forthcoming execution spread like wildfire throughout the community, and Aury knew a huge crowd of spectators would gather for the event, as was common in those days.

Not wanting the humiliation of a public execution, Aury attempted suicide the night before his hanging. While in his jail cell, he managed to slit his throat, but a fast-acting jailer summoned a surgeon who was able to stop the bleeding and stitch up the wound.

The following morning, Aury was led to a scaffold behind the jail. The authorities made sure his shirt collar was buttoned high to conceal his stitches. As expected, an audience had gathered and was in a fever of anticipation, waiting for a show. A noose suspended from a large oak tree was placed around Aury's neck and the trap was released. However, things didn't quite go as planned. When his neck snapped, the stitches ripped loose, and his body was nearly decapitated. A huge, gaping wound in his throat sprayed blood on the horrified onlookers. It was said that men screamed, women fainted, and children nearly got trampled as the crowd backed away from the gruesome scene.

According to Alexander Buell, an associate director at the museum, although it's possible there is some truth to this legend, there is no known documentation to prove the historicity of Luc Simone Aury or the events surrounding his life and death. Furthermore, the Old Jail in which the museum is housed wasn't constructed until 1935. It replaced the original jail which was built in 1878. The alleged hanging of Aury in the 1830s predates the existence of both jails. During that time period, most pirates would have been hanged at the harbor as a warning to other pirates. If the execution did happen in town, it would have been in the center plaza of Old Town Fernandina. Buell points out that the town wasn't built in its present-day location until after 1854, when David Yulee relocated it.

Although this is most likely not the place where Aury was executed, people do claim to see ghastly apparitions of him in and around the Old Jail, and supposedly he still bears an open, bloody gash in his throat. Some people speculate that Aury might have a connection to some artifact housed in the museum that attracts his spirit to this place.

There have also been reports of mysterious moaning sounds near the museum. Employees who work late hours at the museums will sometimes hear disembodied voices. Occasionally the voices will even respond to their questions and answer them. In 2009, the Jacksonville Paranormal Society was brought in to conduct an investigation. They noted some EMF spikes and captured a number of EVPs.

The Palace Saloon

Location: Fernandina Beach, Amelia Island, Nassau County, Florida
Address: 117 Centre Street,
Fernandina Beach, FL 32034-4236
Phone: (904) 491-3332
Website: www.thepalacesaloon.com

Ghost Lore

The Palace Saloon, which officially opened its doors in 1903, has several distinctions. It's Florida's longest operating bar. It was the last saloon to sell alcohol during the Prohibition. It was first bar to serve Coca-Cola. And it's home to Amelia Island's most famous ghost. Charlie Beresford, affectionately known as "Uncle Charlie," lived at the Palace and worked there as a bartender for 54 years. Many people considered him to be a permanent fixture, but it wasn't until after his death that people realized how permanent of a fixture he really was.

- The sound of footsteps is heard upstairs.
- A dishwasher turns on by itself.
- Bar stools fall over.
- Beer taps and faucets turn on by themselves.
- Lights turn on and off.
- The player piano will play on its own . . . while unplugged.
- Trash cans shake and move.
- Glasses mysteriously shatter.
- The door to Uncle Charlie's room opens and closes on its own.
- The presence of Uncle Charlie can be felt in the upstairs rooms.
- Apparitions of Uncle Charlie have been seen near the bar.

History

1878 – The Fernadina Cash Boot and Shoe Store was built on the corner of Centre and 2nd Street by Lt. Josiah G. Prescott (1866-1938).

1901 – On July 3, German immigrant Louis G. Hirth purchased the building for $5,500 and turned it into the Palace Saloon.

1903 – The Palace Saloon officially opened its doors for business.

1905 – Hirth spent $1,400 to decorate the bar with ornate bar fixtures that were hand-carved from black mahogany and English oak.

1906 – Charlie Beresford was hired as a bartender.

1907 – Hirth commissioned Fernandina artist Roy Kennard to paint murals on the walls.

1919 to 1933 – Prohibition. The bar became an ice cream parlor, but continued to sell liquor "under the counter." A brothel was established on the second floor.

1938 – Hirth died and the saloon was operated by the Hirth estate.

1957 – Dee C. Land (1909-1980) and his business partner H. Ervin Willams (1904-1976) purchased the bar from the Hirth estate for $10,000 and spent double that amount to restore it to its original turn-of-the-century splendor.

1960 – Uncle Charlie died.

1960s – Ladies were admitted to the bar for the first time.

1999 – The Palace was damaged by fire, but renovated.

Investigation

According to rumors, Uncle Charlie committed suicide by hanging himself in the back bar of the building. There is no truth to those stories. To set the record straight, Uncle Charlie died peacefully in his sleep in his room at the saloon.

In 1999, when a fire broke out in the Palace Saloon, all the upstairs rooms were damaged, with the exception of the one where Uncle Charlie lived. Most people believe his spirit somehow interceded to protect his apartment from the blaze.

The Palace Saloon was home to Uncle Charlie, and he apparently decided to never leave. Moreover, he wanted to make sure patrons and employees knew he never left; therefore, he gives them constant reminders. Doors will open and close on their own. Beer taps mysteriously turn on. And the player piano plays on its own—while unplugged!

Some of the old-timers at the saloon recall how "Uncle Charlie," had a little racket whereby he bet customers they couldn't toss coins and have them land of the busts of statues behind the bar. After the bar closed, he'd gather up all the change and put it in his tip jar. A few years after his death, another bartender decided to borrow Charlie's idea and started making the same bets with customers, until he felt an invisible hand on his shoulder and knew it was Charlie expressing his disapproval.

Williams House

Location: Fernandina Beach, Amelia Island, Nassau County, Florida
Address: The Amelia Island Williams House, 103 South Ninth Street, Fernandina Beach, FL 32034-3616
Phone: (904) 277-2328
Toll-Free: 1-800-414-9258
Email: info@williamshouse.com
Website: www.williamshouse.com
Innkeepers: Byron and Deborah McCutchen

AMELIA ISLAND CARRIAGES
Phone: (904) 556-2662
Website: www.ameliahorsecarriages.com
Email: info@ameliahorsecarriages.com
Horses: Boomer, Jazz, and Sarge
Owners: Cyndi and Jeff Myers

Ghost Lore

At the insistence of local residents, author Terry Fisk and his wife Jeannine arranged a ghost tour through Amelia Island Carriages, owned and operated by Cyndi and Jeff Myers. The carriage was pulled by Boomer, a beautiful white Percheron (an ancient breed of French draft horse). Boomer, who weighs 2,400 lbs. and stands 19 hands at the shoulder, towered over 5'6" Cyndi. During the tour, Cyndi stopped the carriage to allow an SUV to pass. As it did, curious Boomer turned around to look and was hit in the face by the vehicle. To our astonishment, the accident didn't even faze Boomer, but it ripped the side mirror off the SUV. The ghost tour includes several "snack stops" because of Boomer's insatiable appetite. Whenever the locals saw Boomer coming down the street, it was customary for them to ran out to greet him with an apple or some other treat.

When people visit Amelia Island, we advise them to bring our book and to take the 50-minute carriage tour. Cyndi's knowledge of the history and hauntings of Fernandina Beach is extensive, and the tour includes several ghost stories and haunted locations not discussed in this book. Carriage tours can be arranged through the Williams House or you can contact Amelia Island Carriages directly.

The tour begins at the Williams House, a haunted bed and breakfast, which is a great place to spend the night when you're visiting the island and hoping to see some ghostly action.

- The sounds of children laughing, playing, and singing have been heard, usually upstairs.

- A phantom little girl has been seen.

- Voices have been heard in the parlor.

- Shadows and apparitions have been seen in the mirror.

- The bookcase opens on its own.

- A man wearing a grey suit and fedora has been seen in one of the rooms.

- Candlesticks levitated and flew across the room.

- Faces and apparitions have appeared in photos.

- Blinds will rise on their own.

- Bathroom showers will turn on and off by themselves.

History

1818 – On January 19, Marcellus Alphonso Williams was born in North Carolina.

1836 – On July 16, Emma Michaela Wightman (or Whiteman) was born in Saint Augustine. She was the great-great-granddaughter of the King of Spain.

1847 – Williams moved to Florida.

1854 – On June 19, in the town of Palatka, Marcellus and Emma were wed. They went on to have nine children.

1856 – The house was built by George R. Fairbanks for a wealthy banker from Boston.

1859 – It was purchased by Mr. and Mrs. Williams. They raised a family of nine children: Kate, Arthur, Emma, Herbert, Sallie, Fannie, Marcellus Jr., Edwin, and Farey. New York architect Robert S. Schuyler designed the gingerbread (fret work) surrounding the porches.

1861 – Jefferson Davis, a close friend of Williams', was a frequent houseguest. Ironically, Williams was active in the Underground Railroad, providing a safe house for runaway slaves.

1862 – Union troops seized control of Amelia Island. The Williams family fled to Waldo, Florida, and the Union soldiers used their house as a headquarters and infirmary.

1865 – After the Civil War, the Williams family returned to Fernandina Beach. President Andrew Jackson appointed Mr. Williams as Registrar of the Public Lands for the state of Florida.

1884 – On July 14, Sallie Williams died.

1880 – The south wing was added to the house.

1888 – On July 2, Mr. Williams passed away at the age of 70.

1890 – On February 2, Emma Williams died at the age of 53.

1890 to 1946 – The Williams children lived in the house until the last one died.

1946 – Thomas H. and Gertrude Blatchford bought the house.

1993 – In November, it was purchased by Chris Carter and Dick Flitz. They renovated the house and converted it into a bed and breakfast.

1994 – In May, the Williams House Bed and Breakfast opened for business.

2002 – Paul and Nancy Barnes purchased the inn.

2005 – It was acquired by Byron and Deborah McCutchen.

Investigation

The house was built in 1856 by George R. Fairbanks. Marcellus and Emma Williams purchased the house in 1859 and went on to have nine children. The house and the family were noteworthy for a number of reasons. Mr. Williams was a land surveyor for the Federal Government, and worked for a firm owned by Lawrence

Washington, the nephew of George Washington. Mrs. Williams was the great-great-great-granddaughter of the King of Spain. The Williams family was active in the Underground Railroad and provided a safe house for runaway slaves. There is a trap door in the dining room closet that leads to a secret room where the slaves could hide. Jefferson Davis was a friend of the family and frequent house guest; he also stored his book collection in the house. Dr. Ashbel C. Williams, the grandson of Marcellus and Emma Williams, was a noted oncologist in Jacksonville and later the president of the American Cancer Society. His initials are still carved in the kitchen windowsill.

Chris and Dick. One night, Chris Carter had a dream that he and an older gentleman with blue eyes and grey hair were living in a grand Victorian house with an elegant staircase and chandeliers. Three years later, a realtor showed Chris and his new partner Dick Flitz the historic Williams House in Fernandina Beach. Dick remembers having a strange experience when he first walked into the house. He felt the warm embrace of invisible arms that wel-

Sallie Williams (on the far left) and her siblings.
Photo courtesy of Dick Flitz and Chris Carter.

comed him, and at that moment, he knew he was home. Although the house was in a state of disrepair, the men were confident that it had potential. Without a second thought, the two men bought the house and began renovating it to fulfill their dream of owning a bed and breakfast.

However, within the first couple of weeks, curious things began to happen. The men began to hear strange noises, voices, and the sound of slamming doors in the middle of the night. In the morning, they noticed kitchenware on a kitchen shelf had been rearranged, and some of it had been moved to a different shelf. A bookcase door would be found open. When they closed it and secured the latch, they would return later only to find the door once again wide open. The two men began remodeling the rooms, and noticed their tools would disappear overnight. It seemed as if the spirits in the house came to life once the sun went down. Dick

Ghost image of Sallie on the staircase.
Photo courtesy of Dick Flitz and Chris Carter.

sometimes had a problem with insomnia; on one occasion, in the middle of the night, he went downstairs to the kitchen to use his computer. As he worked quietly, he was suddenly startled to hear a woman's voice and laughter in the same room, yet nobody was there. Walking through the house, he could hear men and women talking in the dining room, and the voices of men in the hallway and parlor.

Their suspicions that the house was haunted were eventually validated. A tour bus had brought a group of people to tour the historic house, and afterwards one of the tourists, who happened to be a psychic, approached Chris, and said she had seen him earlier in the day when he was out walking his golden retriever. According to her, she could see a bright blue aura about him, and informed him he was psychic, but just didn't know it. She also said, "Your house is full of spirits...and they love you!"

A few days later, Chris was cleaning an upstairs bathroom when he heard two or three young girls standing behind him talking and giggling. He stood up and turned around, but nobody was there. Inspecting the hallway, he found it to be empty; when he called out, nobody answered. Two weeks later, he was in the same room when he felt three taps on his shoulder, as if someone was trying to get his attention. He spun around, and again saw nobody there. This time, however, he acknowledged the unseen presence by saying, "I know you're here. I love you, and I'm comfortable with you."

As the renovation was nearing completion, Dick took some photos of the interior of the house and snapped about 15-20 photos of the staircase with its six-foot high mirror. When the photos were developed, he was surprised to see the image of a woman's face reflected in the mirror. He didn't recognize the face, and wondered who she might be.

One day Chris determined the house had a masculine feel to it and decided it needed a masculine name, but he wasn't sure what to call it. The next day the doorbell rang, and the two men greeted a woman who said her aunt, Gertrude Blatchford, used to live in the house. The woman had arrived with a vanload of about ten people.

When she asked for a tour of the house, Chris and Dick were only too happy to oblige. Within the group was a white-haired lady with cane who turned to Chris and said, "Young, man, you know this house has a name. My husband named it 'Beoynathon' after his estate in England." Chris felt this was the masculine name the house wanted to be known by.

A few days later, Gertrude's niece, who was there earlier, returned to visit Chris and Dick. She told them of her mother's love of the house and said, "Mother always said if she could choose her place of death, it would be to die in this house, and if she couldn't do that then she hoped to at least return to it after death." She had brought along a photo of her mother to show the men. When they saw it, they immediately retrieved their photo album to show her the picture of the phantom woman in the mirror. When the woman saw it, her jaw dropped open, her face turned white, and she broke down in tears—the face in the mirror was her mother!

In May of 1994, the renovation was completed, and Chris was walking through the house when he experienced *Déjà vu*. Later, he remembered the dream he had several years ago and realized this was the same house, and Dick was the older gentleman with blue eyes and grey hair that he had dreamed about.

When the inn opened for business, it wasn't just Chris and Dick who experienced the haunting activity; it was also their guests. Chris' brother Wil spent the night in the house, and in the morning he heard the laughter of a young girl on the veranda. Looking out his window, he saw nobody there, but he found himself suddenly drawn to the local cemetery. He gave in to the strange impulse and rode his bike to St. Peter's Episcopal Church Cemetery, and an unseen force pulled him towards a particular grave. He was surprised to discover it was the headstone for Sallie Williams who died July 14, 1884; that day happened to be the anniversary of her death. Was it Sallie that he heard on the veranda that morning?

Dick also had an encounter with young Sallie. While in the dining room refilling glasses of orange juice for his guests, across the hall he saw a little girl standing in the middle of the living room staring up at the mantle. She was about eight-years-old, and wore a long, flowing, white diaphanous dress or nightgown. She "walked" out of the room, but he described her movement as smooth, almost as if she were floating or gliding. She maneuvered around an ice tea cart and approached the staircase. She went to put a foot on the bottom step, then vanished. On a second occasion, he saw her in the grand hall. She looked at him, then nodded. He nodded back, whereupon she smiled and dissolved into thin air.

Guests who stayed at the inn frequently asked to take photographs of the interior of the house, and the owners always granted them permission. One guest later called them to say she was mailing them one of the pictures, but requested they call her before opening the envelope, which they did. What they saw was the photo of a blue apparition of a little girl in a diaphanous dress standing at the top of the staircase. Chris and Dick suspected it was Sallie, and their suspicion was confirmed when Cotton Heines, a descendant of the Williams family, gave them a 1870s photo showing Sallie on the beach at Fort Clinch. It was unmistakably the same girl!

Sallie was not the only family member to die in the house. According to his obituary, Marcellus Williams Jr. died of a heart attack in the house in 1912 at the age of 44; it's believed his spirit still resides there. One night Chris woke up at 2:30 am and saw a middle-aged man standing at the foot of the bed. The man was wearing a grey suit with a matching grey fedora and grey spats. He stood with his arms folded and his head tilted, looking down at Chris. Inexplicably, Chris felt no fear. He sat up and the figure vanished. One week later, several guests spent the night at the inn, and in the morning they were gathered at the breakfast table when one of the women shared a curious experience she had at 2:30 am. She awoke to see a man wearing a grey suit with a matching grey fedora and grey spats standing at the foot of her bed. She was not afraid, though she instinctively knew it was a spirit. Hoping to have a second eyewitness to corroborate her story, she shook her husband to wake him, but it was too late; the specter had disappeared. The woman was unaware that just a few days earlier Chris had experienced an identical manifestation.

Byron and Deborah McCutchen. In 2005, the bed and breakfast was purchased by Byron and Deborah McCutchen, and the haunting activity continued as the couple began to have experiences similar to the previous owners. They would hear doors slamming shut, the bookcase would open, and the blinds would rise on their own.

According to the McCutchens, young Sallie has been seen on the staircase, and she apparently likes to hide things and play little pranks. In the living room, the McCutchens kept two taper candles on the mantle; it was the same mantle that Dick Flitz had seen Sallie staring at. The tapers were securely set in an appropriately designed candleholder, which kept them in an upright position for proper and safe burning. On several occasions the owners were puzzled when they entered the room and found both candles out of their holders and lying in the middle of the living room floor. They kept returning the candles to their holders, but somehow they still ended up on the floor. A few weeks later, the hosts were visiting with guests in the living room when everyone present was astound-

The candlesticks that levitated.

ed to witness both candles levitating straight up out of the holders and fly across the room. The guests exclaimed, "Wow! That's a neat trick! How did you do it?" But the McCutchens were just as perplexed as the guests.

One evening, a woman was staying in the King Ferdinand room at the inn when she heard the classic haunting sound of rattling chains being dragged across the floor of her room. Not one to be intimidated by ghosts, the feisty gal shouted, "You'll have to do more than that to scare me!"

Two young women were staying in the Egmond Indigo Suite. One was very religious, and every morning she would pray on her knees. While giving thanks for being able to stay in the Williams House and for other blessings, the shower suddenly turned on, yet nobody was in the bathroom. Suspecting it was the ghost of Sallie, the disquieted woman shouted, "Hey, that's not funny!" Whereupon the shower shut off.

Deborah relates a story of when she was planning to sing a solo at a wedding, and was in the parlor rehearsing. She was listening to an instrumental recording on a CD and singing along with sheet music when the phone rang. Rushing into the other room to answer the phone, she left the CD playing. While talking on the phone, she became aware that she could hear the voice of a little girl in the parlor, and the girl was singing the same song on the CD. Deborah dropped the phone and ran into the parlor, but nobody was there. Suspecting it was Sallie, she addressed the ghost and said, "Gee, that was pretty." Later when Deborah told Bryon about the strange event, he quipped, "Maybe Sallie wanted to sing a duet."

We recently spoke with Byron and asked if there had been any new activity since the last time we were there. He recounted an event that happened just a few days before when he and Deborah were getting ready to go somewhere. Deborah was in the car waiting for him, and he was running around the house in a frenzied rush, trying to get ready. As he ran out the back door, he heard a deep voice behind him say, "What's the rush?"

The Homestead

Location: Jacksonville Beach, Duval County, Florida
AKA: The Homestead House
Address: 1712 Beach Boulevard,
Jacksonville Beach, FL 32250-2606
Phone: (904) 247-6820
Fax: (904) 246-8743
Email: info@homesteadrestaurant.us
Website: www.homesteadrestaurant.us

Ghost Lore

The Homestead Restaurant might be well-known for its tasty Homestyle Southern cuisine with Cajun influence, but it's even better known for the supernatural atmosphere of the restaurant. It's said that the original owner, Alpha Paynter, was buried in the backyard, yet her spirit remains like a vigilant sentry, watching over the eatery in which she took so much pride.

- Bathroom faucets turn on full blast by themselves.

- Bathroom doors open and close and even lock on their own.

- The bathtub fills up for no reason.

- Lights turn on and off when nobody is around.

- Menus, table linens, and silverware are mysteriously thrown about.

- Items in the kitchen become rearranged.

- Plates inside closed cabinets have been found shattered.

- Candles have lit themselves.

- Disembodied voices, the sound of a woman humming, and other strange noises have been heard.

- Apparitions of a woman looking out of an upstairs window.

- The sound of wine bottles tapping together.

- Water spontaneously flowing out of vases that hold artificial plants.

History

1932 – The two-story pine log cabin was originally built as a private residence.

1934 – The owner left it to Alpha O. Paynter, a radiologist, who converted it into a boarding house.

1947 – Ms. Paynter turned it into a restaurant.

1962 – The restaurant was sold to Preben and Nina Johansen. On Dec. 8, Paynter died at the age of 75 and was allegedly buried in the backyard of the restaurant.

1975 – The Johansens sold the place to Carmen and Steve Macri. They added the bar known as the Copper Top Pub.

2002 – The Macris sold it to Kathy Marvin (the daughter of the Johansens), Malcolm Marvin, and Teresa Brown Pratt.

2007 – North Florida Paranormal Research Inc. (Ghost Trackers) conducted an investigation. After months of bridge and road construction on Beach Boulevard, the owners were forced to close the restaurant and sell it.

2008 – New owners, Abbas and Judy Bagheri, reopened the Homestead.

2010 – Northeast Florida Paranormal Investigations (NEFLPI), accompanied by the crew from CW 17 *Local Haunts*, conducted an investigation.

Investigation

Apparitions of Alpha Paynter have been seen in the bathroom mirror. Sometimes she's seen near the bar or on the staircase or standing at the top of the stairs. On chilly nights, witnesses see her standing near the fireplace and are startled to see her vanish before their eyes. She's usually described as a "lady in white," but sometimes she's wearing a purple dress. Most people describe her as being an older woman.

Employees have been tapped on the shoulder only to turn around and find nobody there. One contractor working alone in the building late at night had this experience and immediately walked off the job, never to return. The staff reported that one morning they came to work and found the tables and chairs had been moved outside the restaurant.

North Florida Paranormal Research Inc., also known as the Ghost Trackers, conducted investigations in 2002 and 2007. They observed an eyeglasses case sitting on a countertop inexplicably fly at one of their investigators. The sound of a woman humming was heard near the Coppertop Bar. It was captured on tape and has been posted on YouTube. A team member also photographed the image of a shadowy figure at the bottom of the staircase.

In 2010, the Northeast Florida Paranormal Investigations (NEFLPI) was given access to the Homestead to conduct a formal investigation. They brought in their equipment and were joined by Steve Christian and Amy Gaston of the *Local Haunts* television series which airs on CW 17 in Jacksonville. Two of the investigators heard a disembodied voice say "go away," and it was captured on tape. They also recorded a number of EVPs. At one point they saw a chair move across the office floor.

We were unable to verify some of the rumors about the Homestead. There are stories circulating about a woman named Angie (some say "Angle") Rosenburg who allegedly committed suicide by hanging herself in the back part of the restaurant. It is alleged that exactly ten years later her daughter Annie hanged herself in a storage closet at the restaurant. Some versions of the story claim this happened in the 1860s, which isn't possible, since the restaurant didn't exist at that time. Other versions claim it happened in the 1960s or '70s, yet we were unable to find any documentation to support that. Some of the stories misidentify Angie Rosenburg as the founder of the restaurant, which leads us to believe she's being confused with Alpha Paynter.

Another rumor is that Alpha Paynter was buried behind the restaurant, but no grave marker can be found there, and it's doubtful that the city would have allowed a burial on private land in 1962. It is possible she was cremated and her ashes were either buried or scattered in the yard.

Casablanca Inn on the Bay

Location: Saint Augustine, Saint Johns County, Florida
Address: 24 Avenida Menendez,
Saint Augustine, FL 32084-3644
Phone: (904) 829-0928
Toll-Free: 1-800-826-2626
Fax: (904) 826-1892
E-mail: innkeeper@casablancainn.com
Website: www.casablancainn.com

Ghost Lore

She's known as "The Lady with the Lantern" or simply the "Hostess" of the haunted Casablanca Inn. Tour guides talk about a former innkeeper who ran a speakeasy here during the Prohibition and assisted rumrunners by waving a lantern to signal their ships when it was safe to smuggle alcohol into the city. Many believe this lantern-swinging ghost lady is still warning phantom ships in the harbor. Some say she still resides in the inn.

- Boaters in the harbor have reported a light flashing on the roof of the inn.

- People on the street have seen a shadowy figure standing on widow's walk as if keeping a vigil. Most times she is swinging a lantern. After a few minutes, she vanishes.

- Guests next door at the Casa de La Paz have also seen the light coming from the roof of the Casablanca Inn.

- Guests at the Casablanca have encountered nebulous apparitions of the woman in the hallways and on the stairs.

- Room 8 is alleged to be the most haunted.

- Cold spots in the rooms.

- Sounds of children playing, voices, and footsteps.

- Objects in guest rooms are moved. Items disappear from suitcases and are later found in unexpected places.

- Some have physically felt her touch.

- One guest claims to have photographed the ghostly woman in the mirror.

History

1914 – The Matanzas Hotel, named after the Matanzas Bay, was built in Mediterranean Revival style. It was designed by Gould T. Butler, one of Henry Flagler's engineers that developed the Florida railroads.

1919 – The Volstead Act was introduced by Andrew J. Volstead to implement the Eighteenth Amendment of the Constitution, which forbade the sale of alcoholic beverages.

1920 to 1933 – Prohibition. Florida became a major nexus of liquor smuggling. The Matanzas Hotel was known as the Bayfront Boarding House and became a speakeasy. The innkeeper was a widow who worked with the rumrunners.

1933 – December 5. The 21st Amendment ended Prohibition and with it the rum-running business. The widow renovated the boarding house into a bed and breakfast.

2005 – The bed and breakfast was purchased by business partners Nancy Cloud and Michael Miles. Nancy, a psychiatric social worker, and Michael, an advertising executive, have been married since 1976.

Investigation

With the beginning of Prohibition in the 1920s, a lucrative opportunity opened up for bootleggers and rumrunners along Florida's Atlantic coast. Booze was smuggled in from Cuba, Jamaica, Puerto Rico, and other Caribbean islands. Treasury agents were assigned to combat the problem.

During this time, the Matanzas Hotel in St. Augustine had become the Bayfront Boarding House, and the proprietor was an elderly widow who ran an inexpensive and well-kept establishment. Frequently the treasury agents would visit St. Augustine in search of rumrunners, and they would always rent rooms at the boarding house.

Times were tough, and when the woman's financial difficulties became overwhelming, she cleverly found a solution to her money problems. Because the federal agents always called ahead to make room reservations before they came to town, she realized she had access to some valuable information. Consequently, the sly woman formed an alliance with the smugglers. For a substantial fee she would warn them whenever the revenuers were in town. In addition, she ran a speakeasy from her inn, providing liquor to her guests and the local townspeople.

The smugglers would normally arrive at dusk and wait in Matanzas Bay for a prearranged signal from the widow. If the agents were not in town, she would climb to the widow's walk on the roof of the inn and wave a lantern back and forth. If the coast wasn't clear, so to speak, they would continue sailing up the coast.

Occasionally the smugglers would stay at the inn, and eventually the woman took one of them as her lover. The romance continued for several years but had a tragic ending. One day the bootleggers sailed into the bay, but the treasury agents were staying at the boarding house. Her boyfriend waited patiently in the harbor for the signal to come ashore, but sadly he died at sea when a hurricane blew in. The woman was grief-stricken for years thereafter.

By the time Prohibition had been repealed in 1933, the woman had become a millionaire from her illegitimate business. She later converted the boarding house into the Casablanca Inn Bed and Breakfast and died shortly after. Rumor has it that she was buried in the Huguenot Cemetery, but this is refuted by the fact that the last burial in the cemetery was in 1884. Although the identity of the widow is known, she remains anonymous in deference to her relatives who still live in the city.

Since her death, fishermen and shrimpers in the harbor have seen a light emanating from the roof of the Casablanca Inn on moonless nights. Some have reported it to authorities thinking it was a signal for help, but no source for the light could ever be found. People walking past the inn will also sometimes see it. Some even claim to see a shadowy figure on the roof swinging a lantern back and forth. After a few minutes, she vanishes before their eyes.

Guests staying at the Casa de La Paz next door will sometimes be awakened late at night because of a light shining in their window. Their first thought is that it's the lighthouse on Anastasia Island, but they quickly discover the light is shining from the roof of the Casablanca Inn and appears to be a lantern.

There is a great deal of speculation as to why the "Hostess" haunts the inn. Some see the eternally repetitive action of swinging the lantern as a Sisyphean task—requital for her illegal activities. Most think the phantom widow still grieves for her lost lover and hopes he will see her signal and come back to the inn to spend eternity with her.

Castillo de San Marcos

Location: Saint Augustine, Saint Johns County, Florida
Address: 1 South Castillo Drive,
Saint Augustine, FL 32084-3252
Phone: (904) 829-6506
Fax: (904) 823-9388

Ghost Lore

Castillo de San Marcos is the oldest masonry fort in the continental United States. Its name literally means "The Castle of St. Mark," and just like a medieval castle, it has a moat with a drawbridge and a portcullis. But that's not where the similarities end. Like most castles, this one also has its share of ghosts.

- At night, people have seen a light coming from one of the small windows next to one of the fireball ovens.

97

- The scent of a woman's perfume, either patchouli or orange blossom.

- The odor of garlic mingled with sweat.

- The decapitated head of Osceola has been seen floating around the fort.

- Apparitions of a Spanish soldier who appears to be searching for a lost ring.

- A phantom guard who reeks of garlic and sweat is seen in one of the watchtowers.

- A mysterious cloaked figure is seen standing on the same watchtower. He has an intense look in his eyes and stares into the bay. It's believed he was a pirate who was hanged at the fort, and eternally awaits the return of his shipmates.

- A woman in a white dress wanders the grounds of the fort. When approached, she vanishes into the trees or the walls.

History

1565 – The settlement of St. Augustine was founded by Spain under Admiral Pedro Menéndez de Avilés. Over the next century, the city was protected by a succession of nine wooden forts.

1586 – St. Augustine was sacked by Sir Francis Drake.

1668 – The settlement was plundered by English pirate Robert Searles. Because of these attacks, Mariana of Austria (1634-1696), the Queen consort of Spain, authorized the construction of a fort to protect the city.

1672 – The Spanish began construction on Castillo de San Marcos. As a building material, workers used coquina from Anastasia Island. Coquina is a type of stone made up of sea shells.

1695 – After 23 years of labor, construction of the fortification was completed.

1702 – British troops attacked St. Augustine. The city's residents and the Spanish troops took shelter in the Castillo. The British cannonballs bounced off the coquina walls, and the fort held strong. After a two-month long attack, the British were eventually driven off by the Spanish fleet.

1740 – After the British declared war on Spain, British General James Oglethorpe attacked the Castillo and the city of St. Augustine. Again, after 37 days of bombardment, the British retreated after failing to penetrate the walls of the Castillo.

1825 to 1942 – Florida became a territory of the United States. The fort was renamed Fort Marion.

1837 – Osceola was captured near St. Augustine.

1738 – The fort was renovated.

1739 – The British made another failed attack on the fort.

1763 – The British acquired the fort as part of the Treaty of Paris and changed its name to Fort St. Mark.

1775 to 1783 – During the American Revolution, the British used the fort as a military prison to hold revolutionary fighters who were captured in Charleston.

1784 – The second Treaty of Paris returned the fort to Spain, and they renamed it Castillo de San Marcos.

1819 – The Adams-Onis Treaty ceded Florida to the U.S. The fort was renamed Fort Marion.

1837 – During the Second Seminole War, the fort was used as a prison, housing several Native Americans, including Osceola.

1861 – During the Civil War, Florida ceded from the Union. Union troops abandoned the fort but left one person behind as the caretaker. He peacefully surrendered the fort to Confederate troops, then requested a written receipt, which he received.

1870s and 1880s – The fort was used as a prison for Indians captured by the U.S.

1899 – The fort was no longer used by the U.S. military.

1924 – The fort was designated a National Monument.

1933 – Control of the fort was transferred from the War Department to the National Park Service and became a popular tourist attraction.

1942 – The original name of Castillo de San Marcos was restored.

1966 – It was listed on the National Register of Historic Places.

Investigation

Osceola. During the Second Seminole War, the great Indian warrior Osceola was captured and imprisoned at the fort. During his captivity he contracted malaria and was treated by Dr. Frederick Weedon. Later, Osceola was transported to Fort Moultrie in Charleston, South Carolina and died there on July 30, 1838. Dr. Weedon traveled to Charleston to perform the autopsy and attend the funeral. During the autopsy, he secretly decapitated the warrior and put a scarf around his neck to hide the incision marks. Osceola was respected by both his fellow Indians and by the U.S. military. In fact, he was given a burial with full military honors. Before the casket was buried, Dr. Weedon stealthfully stole the severed head of Osceola, placed it in a bag, and brought it with him back to St. Augustine. The doctor used it to make a death mask, which was a common practice in that day. Later, he embalmed the head and kept it preserved in a jar. According to his children, whenever they misbehaved, as a punishment he would pull the head out of the jar and stick it on their bedpost. The terrified children would have to spent the entire night in bed with the ghastly head looking at them.

We were concerned that the head was never given a proper burial, so we tried to track down its whereabouts. What we found was that the doctor later put the head on display for several years in his pharmacy. When he died, his daughter inherited it. She wanted nothing to do with it, so she donated it to a surgeon in New York. He, in turn, gave it to the Medical College of New York City. They kept it in a museum until 1866 when the museum was razed by fire and the head was destroyed.

Witnesses claim to see the ghostly severed head of Osceola floating through the fort at night. Perhaps the restless spirit is searching for the burial place of the rest of his body.

Don Carlos. During the conflict known as the War of Jenkins' Ear,   Britain declared war on Spain. In 1940, British General James Oglethorpe landed his troops on Anastasia Island across the inlet from St. Augustine with plans of firing on the Castillo. That night, Don Carlos, a young Spanish soldier was off duty and searching for his family ring that he had lost the night before while on patrol. Oglethorpe's first volley on the fort hit him square in the chest, killing him instantly. Over the years, several people have seen the phantom soldier walking in the same spot where he died. They say he appears to be searching frantically for his lost ring. When people approach him, he responds in Spanish.

The Secret Dungeon. In 1784, Colonel Garcia Martí, and his young, attractive wife Señora Delores Martí, came to St. Augustine, and he assumed command of the fort. Delores was unhappy in her marriage and it wasn't long before she initiated a secret affair with Captain Manuela Abela. Colonel Martí was unsuspecting until one day when he had Abela in his office and they were looking over some maps. Martí caught the unmistakable scent of his wife's orange-blossom scented perfume wafting from Abela's uniform.

In a fit of rage, the Colonel plotted his vengeance. Reminiscent of the immurement scene from Edgar Allan Poe's *The Cask of Amontillado,* Martí chained the adulterous couple to a wall in a small room used to store gunpowder, then bricked up the entrance with a coquina wall, sealing them in forever. To explain their disappearance, Colonel Martí told people his wife had taken ill and was staying with family in Mexico and Captain Abela was on a mission in Cuba.

Nobody was the wiser until July 21, 1833. During a renovation of the fort, a Sgt. Tuttle was moving a canon on the gun deck when the floor cracked, and the canon fell through. Underneath, Tuttle and his men found the secret room partially exposed and noticed the sweet scent of orange blossom perfume. The soldiers used tools to chip through the wall and inside they discovered the bones of Señora Delores and Captain Abela.

Since the gruesome discovery, people have seen mysterious lights floating near the dungeon, and they continue to smell the perfume. Often people will see apparitions of a woman wandering the fort at night, and in her wake is the sweet scent of orange blossoms.

The Dare. If you put your ear up to the walls of the fort, you will hear battle sounds such as cannons, gunshots, and soldiers shouting.

103

Huguenot Cemetery

Location: Saint Augustine, Saint Johns County, Florida
Address: The St. Augustine Visitor Information Center,
10 South Castillo Drive, Saint Augustine, FL 32084-3201
Parking: Safe and inexpensive parking is available at the
Historic District Parking Lot located at the Visitor Information
Center.

Directions: Thorough information and directions to downtown
attractions are available at the Visitor Information Center.

Ghost Lore

In 1821, Saint Augustine experienced a devastating epidemic of
yellow fever that killed hundreds of people. Many of the dead were
thrown into mass graves in the newly established Huguenot
Cemetery. To this day, the dead have remained restless.

- Judge Stickney wanders the cemetery late at night in search of his gold teeth taken by grave robbers. Some describe him as sad or angry. Sometimes he's seen sitting up on a branch in a cedar tree that overlooks his grave.

- After midnight, "Little Elizabeth" can be seen standing at the City Gates waving to passersby. Uncertain if she's greeting people or warning them to stay away. Sometimes she's seen dancing in the cemetery. More than once people have called the police after seeing her.

- Unexplained figures, faces, shadows, and lights appear in photographs taken at the cemetery.

- People hear voices and footsteps.

- Ghost children are seen playing in the cemetery and sitting on tombstones.

- Three prankster spirits haunt the cemetery and enjoy pestering people by tipping hats, tapping shoulders, tugging on clothing, grabbing legs, and shoving people.

History

1821 – In July, Florida became a U.S. Territory. In September, there was a yellow fever epidemic in St. Augustine. Judge Thomas Fitch was the first to die. The city established a half acre of land outside the city gates as the Protestant cemetery. It was later named the Huguenot Cemetery after the sixteenth-century French Huguenots massacred by Menéndez.

1825 – Rev. Thomas Alexander purchased the cemetery.

1832 – Rev. Alexander deeded the cemetery to the Trustees of the Presbyterian Church.

1832 – On May 25, John Buffington Stickney was born in Lynn, Massachusetts.

1835 – John Gifford Hull, Erastus Nye, and John Lyman died in January and were buried side-by-side with nearly identical headstones.

1860s – John B. Stickney, then a widower with three young children, moved to St. Augustine and served as the judge for St. Johns County.

1880 – Stickney was appointed as the U.S. Attorney for the Northern District of Florida.

1882 – On Nov. 5, Judge Stickney died of typhoid fever and was buried in the Huguenot Cemetery.

1884 – In August, the cemetery had its last burial. After that, it fell into a long period of neglect.

1903 – Judge Stickney's body was moved to Washington, D.C.

1946 – Cleanup and restoration by concerned citizens.

1951 – Cleanup and restoration by the City of St. Augustine.

1979 – Cleanup and restoration.

1989 – The Cemetery Restoration Committee of Memorial Presbyterian Church was formed.

1993 – The cemetery was taken over by the Friends of the Huguenot Cemetery.

Investigation

John B. Stickney. Judge Stickney lived in St. Augustine and was well-known and liked. He was serving as the U.S. Attorney for the Northern District of Florida when he died of typhoid fever while on a business trip to Washington, D.C. His body was transported by train back to St. Augustine and buried in the Huguenot Cemetery.

Years later, Judge Stickney's three adult children, having relocated to Washington, D.C., decided to have his remains reinterred closer to them. After the gravedigger unearthed the coffin, he either fell asleep or took a break. While the casket sat unguarded, drunken graverobbers took advantage of the situation, smashing the judge's skull and stealing his gold teeth.

To this day, people have seen the forlorn judge wandering through the cemetery wearing a tall hat and a long, black cape. He strolls back and forth, eternally searching for his missing teeth. Curiously, sometimes he's seen sitting in a tree, overlooking his former grave.

Elizabeth. The guard who stood at the City Gate had a young daughter named Elizabeth. During the day, she loved to stand at the gate and greet people. When she was 14 years old, she was the first to die of yellow fever during the epidemic, and her body was dropped off at the cemetery.

It's said that after midnight she can still be seen standing near the City Gate waving. Some believe she's waving to greet people; others believe she's waving to warn people to stay away due to the plague. Other times she's seen inside the cemetery dancing and playing, apparently oblivious of the fact that she's dead.

Prankster Spirits. Three mischievous men—John Hull, Erastus Ny, and John Lyman—died around the same time and were buried in similar graves. It's believed they have returned from the dead to play practical jokes on the living. They have been known to trip people, knock hats off, and even lift up the skirts of young ladies.

Ripley's Believe It or Not! Museum

Location: Saint Augustine, Saint Johns County, Florida
Address: 19 San Marco Avenue,
Saint Augustine, FL 32084-3278
Phone: (904) 824-1606
Email: staugmail@ripleys.com
Website: www.staugustine-ripleys.com

Ghost Lore

When you think of the Ripley's Believe It or Not! Museums, you usually think of oddities such as shrunken heads or the world's largest rubber band ball, but you don't usually think of ghosts. Not so at this museum. One of the displays talks about a mysterious fire that happened in the building years ago when it operated as the Castle Warden Hotel. Two women died in the blaze, and many believe they haunt the museum—believe it or not!

108

- From 1944-46, guests at the Castle Warden Hotel saw apparitions of the women who died in the hotel fire.

- From 1950 to the present, employees of the museum have also seen the apparitions.

- Spectral figures have been seen in the building late at night.

- Ghosts of the women have been seen standing in the windows on the third floor and at the penthouse window on the fourth floor.

- Unexplained sounds of doors slamming, footsteps, and women's voices.

- The sound of furniture being dragged across the second floor, where there are only huge display cases but no moveable furniture.

- Music, particularly the sound of stringed instruments, has been heard in the room that was once the music room. Music has also been heard in the lobby.

- Sounds of a woman sobbing coming from the second floor and sometimes the lobby.

- People have smelled smoke.

- The gift shop is always picked up and organized when the employees closed up for the night, but often they will return the next day to discover merchandise has been rearranged. Employees have seen books fly off the shelves and cash registers open on their own.

- In the theater, tour guides and guests will sometimes be overcome with nausea and dizziness. Psychics claim two spirits occupy that room. People have seen shadowy figures and a mysterious light there.

- Cold spots.

- Sense of anxiety and feeling of being watched.

- A mysterious black shadow has been seen moving through the circus room.

- The Buddha statue in the lobby will be found on its side or change position.

- Doors will open on their own.

- A video display in the museum will sometimes turn itself on . . . even when it's unplugged.

- A ghost woman appeared in a photo taken by a visitor to the museum. The ghost appears to be standing next to a replica of Robert Wadlow, the world's tallest man.

- Tourists find mysterious orbs and streaks of light in photos taken there.

History

1887 – The Warden Winter House was built for the William G. Warden family.

1925 – The house was still owned by the Warden family, but sat vacant for the next sixteen years.

1941 – It was purchased by Norton Baskin and remodeled as the Castle Warden Hotel. He and his wife, Marjorie Kinnan Rawlings, lived in a penthouse apartment on the top floor.

1942 – In April, the Castle Warden Hotel officially opened.

1943 – During World War II, Baskin enlisted and was stationed overseas in Burma as an ambulance driver.

1944 – April 24. A fire broke out in the hotel. Two women, Bette Nevi Richeson and Ruth Hopkins Pickering, died of smoke inhalation.

1946 – Baskin sold the hotel at a profit.

1948 – The hotel closed.

1949 – May 27. Cartoonist Robert Ripley died at the age of 58. His family purchased the hotel to house the many strange artifacts he collected over the years.

1950 – The building opened as the world's first Ripley's Believe It or Not! Museum.

1999 to 2003 – TBS aired the *Ripley's Believe It or Not!* television series, hosted by Dean Cain. Segments of the program were filmed here, including the opening credits.

2009 – Three stars of the Syfy Network's *Ghost Hunters* show conducted a paranormal investigation of the museum.

Investigation

The Warden Winter House. In 1887, a single-family house was built for Philadelphia millionaire William G. Warden (1831-1895) and his family of fourteen children. The house had nineteen family bedrooms and five servant bedrooms, and was designed and built by the Carriere and Hastings firm. Warden was a business partner with John D. Rockefeller and Henry Flagler in the Standard Oil Company.

Castle Warden Hotel. The Warden family lived in the house until 1925. Although the family still owned the house after that, it sat vacant for sixteen years until it was purchased in 1941 by Norton Baskin (1901-1997) and remodeled as the Castle Warden Hotel. His wife, Marjorie Kinnan Rawlings (1896-1953), was the Pulitzer Prize-winning author of *The Yearling* and *Cross Creek*. Both her novels were later made into motion pictures. The couple moved into a penthouse apartment on the top floor, and the following year the hotel opened with 25 guest rooms.

World War II was in progress, and in 1943 Norton Baskin enlisted with the American Field Service, an American volunteer ambulance service that operated under British officers. He ended up being stationed in Burma as an ambulance driver.

While Mr. Baskin was overseas, Mrs. Rawlings lived at her cottage in Cross Creek, as it afforded her the isolation and quiet she needed to write. In St. Augustine, she belonged to a heavy-drinking bridge-playing group along with a close friend, Ruth Hopkins Pickering (age 49). Pickering, who lived just a few blocks from the Castle Warden Hotel on Magnolia Avenue, had an abusive husband. For her safety, Mrs. Rawlings had her move into the fourth floor penthouse suite at the hotel.

On April 24, 1944, a fast-spreading fire broke out in the hotel and swept through the third and fourth floors. Pickering was trapped in her room. She ran to her window and screamed for help, but bellhops were unable to enter her room because of the heat, and she died of smoke inhalation. Another woman, Bette Nevi Richeson, a twenty-something dress shop operator from Jacksonville, was staying on the third floor in a hotel room directly below Pickering's suite. Richeson, who had checked in just 90 minutes before the fire began, also died of inhalation. The deadly infernal, which damaged the third and fourth floors before being contained, was assumed to be an accident caused by a careless smoker; however, some believe it was arson and murder at the hands of Pickering's abusive husband. The true cause of the fire remains a mystery to this day. Mrs. Rawlings grieved her friend's death and felt guilty about it, since the penthouse lacked a fire escape and was acknowledged to be a fire trap. The damage was quickly repaired, and the hotel was sold a couple years later.

Ripley's Believe It or Not! Museum. On May 27, 1949, the cartoonist Robert Ripley died at the age of 58. He was famous for his *Ripley's Believe It or Not!* newspaper comic which had 80 million readers worldwide. Mr. Ripley had owned three homes, one of which was his winter home in Palm Beach. Although he had never lived in St. Augustine, he was a frequent guest at the Castle Warden Hotel and thought it would make an ideal location to showcase the collection of oddities he had accumulated from his journeys to 198 countries. Plans for the museum were in the process of being drafted at the time of his death. The following year, his heirs purchased the property and opened the world's first Ripley's Believe It or Not! Museum.

Not long after the museum opened, visitors and employees began to notice strange activity. Apparitions of women were seen in windows on the third and fourth floors. Gift shop employees would find merchandise had been moved around overnight. People were hearing unexplained voices and footsteps, and there were sightings of shadowy figures moving throughout the building.

In 2009, three stars of the Syfy Network's *Ghost Hunters* series visited the museum to conduct a paranormal investigation. Dave Tango, Steve Gonsalves, and Dustin Pari of The Atlantic Paranormal Society (TAPS.) encountered a moving shadowy figure, cold spots, and EMF meter spikes.

Saint Augustine Lighthouse

Location: Saint Augustine, Anastasia Island, Saint Johns County, Florida
Address: Saint Augustine Lighthouse & Museum, 81 Lighthouse Avenue, Saint Augustine, FL 32080-4650
Phone: (904) 829-0745
Email: info@staugustinelighthouse.com
Website: www.staugustinelighthouse.com

Ghost Lore

For centuries, lighthouses have shined a beacon to guide sailors on a safe journey. A popular superstition among mariners is that lighthouses also attract the souls of men who perished at sea. The lighthouse on Anastasia Island is legendary for being a guiding light that has attracted an inordinate number of ghosts. Some have proclaimed it to be the most haunted lighthouse in the world.

LIGHTHOUSE

- Smell of cigar smoke.

- Moving shadows.

- Sound of footsteps on the stairs.

- Voices and strange sounds.

- Flickering lights.

- A phantom woman seen on the stairs.

- Researchers and visitors have recorded photographic anomalies and EVPs.

- Apparitions of two little girls on the catwalk.

- Apparitions of a pretty woman wearing a white dress has been seen standing on the catwalk late at night. She has long black hair that reaches to her waist. Witnesses say she has a sad expression on her face and is usually gazing towards the northwest.

- Apparitions of a lighthouse keeper who fell to his death while painting the tower.

OUTSIDE

- Smell of cigar smoke.

- Icy cold breeze on hot days.

- Sound of young girls playing and giggling.

- Feeling of being followed.

- Apparitions of a girl who was killed by a nearby train.

- A phantom woman seen walking in the yard.

- Apparitions of thirteen pirates who were executed and buried on this site.

- A cigar-smoking ghost seen near the fuel house.

- Apparitions of a lighthouse keeper who drowned nearby.

- At night, people have heard the sounds of footsteps in gravel and walking up the metal spiral staircase in tower.

KEEPER'S HOUSE MUSEUM

- Cold spots.

- Sound of footsteps on the stairs.

- A sense of being watched.

- Misty grey apparition of a man seen walking the second floor of the house.

- A maintenance worker saw a heavy bench levitate two feet into the air and float across the room.

- Apparitions of a little girl. Sometimes she's seen looking out the window. Other times she's wandering the hallways. Guests sleeping in the second story bedroom have awakened to see her standing in the room.

- Apparitions of a man swinging by a noose from the rafters.

- Apparitions of a man wearing Victorian clothing.

- Apparitions of a man in the basement. He's believed to be one of the original lighthouse keepers.

VISITOR'S CENTER

- Haunted by a ghost referred to as "Albert." Supposedly he died in the house years ago.

- Merchandise and chairs get moved around overnight.

- Music boxes play by themselves.

History

1565 – Pedro Menendez founded St. Augustine. A 35-foot wooden watch tower was built on the north end of Anastasia Island.

1737 – The Spanish converted an old stone chapel and tower into a watchtower.

1824 – The U.S. added a beacon to the top of the watchtower and it became Florida's first official lighthouse. Juan Andreau, a Minorcan, was the first lighthouse keeper.

1859 – On December 5th, Andreu was painting the lighthouse tower and accidentally fell to his death.

1860s – The foundation of the tower was deteriorating.

1871 – Construction of the current lighthouse began. It was designed by Paul Pelz, one of the architects for the Library of Congress in Washington, D.C. Hezekiah H. Pittee of Maine was the superintendent of the construction project.

1873 – Three children, two of whom were daughters of Pittee, died in a tragic accident during the construction.

1874 – The construction was completed. On October 15, the keeper extinguished the light in the old lighthouse, and they began using the new one. At that time it was one of the tallest in the U.S. Lard was used as a fuel for the lamp.

1876 – The lighthouse keeper's two-story, brick house was constructed.

1885 – The keeper began using kerosene to fuel the light in the lamp.

1901 to 1924 – Peter Rasmussen served as the light keeper.

1930s – A man supposedly hanged himself in the house.

1936 – The light was powered by electricity.

1955 – The lighthouse became automated. Chief James L. Pippin was the last keeper to serve. The house was rented out.

1967 – The house was boarded up and sat vacant.

1970 – On July 28th, arsonists set a fire that damaged the light-house and destroyed the interior of the house. The following year, St. Johns County purchased the house. It was vandalized and fell into disrepair while it sat empty.

1980 to 1988 – The Junior Service League of St. Augustine reno-vated the house.

1981 – The lighthouse and the keeper's quarters was listed on the National Register of Historic Places.

1990 to 1994 – The Junior Service League restored the lighthouse tower.

1994 – The Lighthouse Museum of St. Augustine opened to the public.

Investigation

It's one of the world's most famous haunted lighthouses. Everyone from PBS to Discovery Channel to *Ghost Hunters* has been there to conduct an investigation or to do a story. While the majority of the places we investigate have only one ghostly resident, this one boasts of multiple spooks.

Lorina Alcontera. In *Florida Ghost Stories*, author Robert R. Jones claims the lighthouse is haunted by Lorina Alcontera, a young woman who died at the age of 18 about 150 years ago. He recounts two versions of how she supposedly died. In the first story, she leapt to her death from the lighthouse catwalk after hearing of the death of her lover, Roberto, who was killed by Indians near Picalata on the St. Johns River. In the second story, Roberto was murdered by Juan Valdez, a suitor who was also interested in the young woman. As the story goes, Lorina was standing on the catwalk watching for the return of Robert when she was approached by Juan. He informed her of Roberto's death and made advances towards her. In her efforts to escape, she accidentally fell from the top of the lighthouse and was killed. A few days later, Juan died in a shipwreck when his schooner ran aground on a sandbar during a storm. Since her death, people have seen Lorina's apparition standing on the lighthouse catwalk. They describe her as a pretty girl in a white dress, with long black hair and a forlorn expression. She's always gazing off towards the northwest, as if she's still searching and waiting for the return of her long-lost lover.

The Hanged Man. The story is told of a St. Augustine mariner who lost his entire life's savings in the stock market crash of 1929. Penniless and homeless, he resorted to living on the beach near the lighthouse. The lighthouse keeper, Clarence Malloy, was in the lighthouse tending to the light when the man entered his house and hanged himself by the wooden rafters. Years later, visitors to the house have reported seeing his lifeless body dangling by a noose. After their initial shock, the apparition quickly vanishes before their eyes. Although this story could be true, we have been unable to find any documentation to confirm that a suicide actually occurred in the house.

Cigar Smoking Ghost. One of the lighthouse keepers, Peter Rasmussen, habitually smoked cigars. Most photos of him depict him with a cigar in his mouth, and that's how most people remembered him. The only times he didn't smoke were when he was in the house. Mrs. Rasmussen didn't enjoy the smell of the cigars and insisted he smoke them outside. To this day, people will still catch a whiff of his cigar smoke. Occasionally, people will even catch a glimpse of the keeper himself standing outside enjoying a good cigar, then the spirit vanishes into a mist along with the tobacco aroma.

Another theory is that the phantom is a cigar-smoking worker who was painting the lighthouse tower and fell to his death. That's certainly a possibility.

The Little Girls. The lighthouse that currently stands on this location was designed by Paul Pelz, famous for being one of the architects for the Library of Congress in Washington, D.C. Hezekiah H. Pittee of Maine was hired as the superintendent of the construction project. Construction began in 1871, but when the work was taking longer than expected, Pittee decided to move his wife and five children from Maine to an on-site house in St. Augustine.

Tracks were laid from the lighthouse to the beach, and the workers used a railroad handcart to transport building materials from ships up to the work area. Pittee's children frequently played in the cart, but on July 10, 1873, their play ended in tragedy. On that fateful day, five children were playing in the cart, when one of them accidentally released the brake, and it rushed headlong down the track and crashed into the ocean. Workers were able to save a young boy and a girl, but two of Pittee's daughters, Mary (15) and Eliza (13), and a young black girl (7) drowned. A few months later, workers could hear the sounds of children laughing and playing near the lighthouse. Concerned that the surviving children might again be playing near the handcart, they rushed to chase them away, but found nobody there. The voices of the dead children can still be occasionally heard near the lighthouse late at night. Sometimes the phantom children have even been seen standing on the catwalk or near the lighthouse. The ghost of Mary has also been seen in the house. Witnesses describe her as wearing a blue dress and blue bow in her hair, which is what she wore the day she died.

Spanish Military Hospital

Location: Saint Augustine, Saint Johns County, Florida
AKA: The Hospital of Our Lady of Guadalupe
Address: Ancient City Tours, Incorporated, 3 Aviles Street, Saint Augustine, FL 32084-4404
Phone: (904) 825-6808 or (904) 827-0807
Fax: (904) 827-0590
Email: ancientcitytours@bellsouth.net
Website: www.spanishmilitaryhospital.com

Ghost Lore

The Spanish Military Hospital is a reconstruction of a military hospital that once stood on this site during the Second Spanish Colonial Period. The scalpels, bullet retractors, and bone saws on display are the horrific reminders of the agonizing surgeries and amputations that patients endured in this place. It's a place where hundreds of people experienced grisly deaths. But some say even death couldn't bring peace to these tormented souls.

121

- Cold spots.

- Strange smells, especially in the "medicine room."

- Movement of objects.

- The sense of being watched and followed.

- Most haunting activity happens in the recovery room area.

- Shadows have been spotted all throughout the hospital.

- People have reported being touched by an unseen force.

- Guests have captured orbs, strange lights, and other anomalies in photographs taken during the tour.

- A female spirit resides on the second floor and supposedly does not like other females.

- Scratches which form words have appeared on visitor's backs.

- The sound of footsteps.

- A bucket in the ward room slid across the room.

- Apparition of a one-legged man.

- Rapping sounds on the doors and walls.

- People have been touched, scratched and even bitten on more than one occasion.

- Apparitions have been seen inside and outside the building.

- Doors open and close by themselves. They also lock and unlock on their own.

- Objects have been thrown at people.

- A demon who resides in the upstairs office area scratches people.

- Visitors have been struck in the head and on their back by an invisible entity.

History

1784 – The Treaty of Paris allowed Spain to take control of St. Augustine from the British. The Spanish Military Hospital was built that same year.

1821 – With the signing of the Adams-Onis Treaty, Spain sold the Territory of Florida to the United States, and the Spaniards left St. Augustine. The hospital was demolished that same year.

1965 – A reconstruction was built on the original site.

1970s – While repairing waterlines under the street, workers discovered hundreds of human skeletons buried next to the hospital.

Investigation

While walking up to the Spanish Military Hospital, we had no idea as to what we were walking into . . . or walking *over.* The curator explained to us that in the 1970s a leaky water pipe caused the cobblestone street in front of the hospital to cave in. The city sent out a repair crew, and while digging up the street to repair the damage they were horrified when they unexpectedly unearthed hundreds of human skeletons. According to historians, at one time there was a trench dug alongside the hospital, and it was in this mass grave that the surgeons disposed of dead bodies and amputated limbs. The workers hastily replaced the water pipes, then carefully returned the bones to their original burial place before repairing the street.

Needless to say, this hospital is a place of restless spirits. Because of the intensity of its haunting activity, it has attracted numerous ghost hunting teams, and none of them has ever left disappointed.

Peace River Ghost Tracker. When this team visited in 2005, they captured orbs on videotape, EVPs, and EMF spikes. One of the team members experienced an unexplained numbness in his mouth. Later in the apothecary, they noticed a bottle of clove oil on a table. Upon inspecting the bottle, they discovered that it was wet beneath it. Dentistry was practiced at the hospital, and clove oil would have been used to numb the patient's mouth.

During a second investigation in 2009, one of the members reclined on a hospital bed in the mourning room, attempting to invoke a response from a ghost by pretending to be a patient. He was startled when an invisible hand gently squeezed his. The group also encountered hot spots, cold spots, and unexplained knocking sounds.

Ghost Tracker. When the Orlando-based WJXT television series *Ghost Tracker* investigated the hospital, they reportedly saw a heavy bed levitate off the floor, and later had a conversation with a 15-year-old Spanish soldier.

Northeast Florida Paranormal Investigations. This team said they could definitely feel some type of presence in the building. They heard strange noises, and their equipment picked up EVPs and photographic and video anomalies.

HGWI (Historic Ghost Watch and Investigation). When the HGWI team was there in 2005, they had a variety of interesting experiences. Initially, they had the usual equipment malfunctions,

which are so common on ghost investigations. One camera went off by itself. Later walkie-talkies and cameras quit working. They were, however, able to catch some EMF spikes. The team encountered cold spots and cold drafts, and at times it was cold enough to experience goosebumps. Their instruments recorded temperatures drops anywhere from 4 to 5 degrees. The investigators heard a variety of strange sounds: tapping or ticking, a little girl's voice, footsteps, raspy breathing, a male whisper, rustling, and the sound of heavy furniture being dragged across a floor. In one room they sensed the strong odor of excrement or sewage. Mysterious white lights were seen moving through the room, and orbs were captured on video. However, the most impressive events of the night happened in the downstairs office. Within the office, they saw a bathroom door shut on its own. After leaving the office and venturing into an adjoining room, they heard the sound of a deadbolt being locked. The sound was even captured on tape. Later they found the office door shut, and the deadbolt was locked...from the inside.

R.I.P. (Researchers Investigating the Paranormal). R.I.P. found the spirits to be extremely active during their investigation. The team heard unexplained banging and popping noises. One investigator felt the invisible hand of a small child touch their arm. Another had their hair yanked by an unseen hand; simultaneously, an EVP was recorded saying, "don't go!" The most spectacular event was when the team watched a dime slide of its own accord across a table.

NORTHWEST FLORIDA

Coombs House Inn

Location: Apalachicola, Franklin County, Florida
Address: 80 Sixth Street, Apalachicola, FL 32320-1750
Phone: (850) 653-2634 or (850) 653-9199
Toll-Free: 1-888-244-8320
Fax: (850) 653-2785
Email: info@coombshouseinn.com
Website: www.coombshouseinn.com
Innkeepers: Scott & Ana Wilson
Resident Innkeeper: Estella Banta

Ghost Lore

Often it seems that renovating an older house will stir up the spirits, and houses that previously had no reported haunting activity are suddenly "alive" with all kinds of restless spirits. What's unique about the Coombs House Inn is that one of the carpenters who worked on the renovation has apparently returned to haunt the inn.

- A phantom handyman has been seen.

- The ghost of timber tycoon James N. Coombs still resides in the house.

- A ghost will sometimes softly caress guests sleeping at the inn.

- Mysterious sounds of children laughing and playing have been heard coming from empty rooms.

- An unexplained phantom balloon has floated through the house.

- The ghosts of two woman—one older and the other younger—have been seen in the attic.

- The house has several cold spots.

History

1842 – On August 15, James Nathaniel Coombs was born in Oldtown, Maine. His parents were I. W. and Malinda Parker Coombs. His father was in the saw mill business.

1862 to 1863 – James N. Coombs served in the Union Army during the Civil War. He was as a Sergeant in the 28th Maine Regiment.

1866 – On April 10, he married his childhood sweetheart, 19-year-old Maria A. Starrett, the daughter of Abner and Mary Starrett.

1871 – The couple moved from Maine to Pensacola, Florida, and Coombs was successful in the lumber business.

1877 – When the supply of trees in that region was exhausted, the couple moved to Apalachicola, Florida. Coombs' business flourished, and he became a wealthy and influential lumber baron.

1900 – Coombs, a member of the Republican Party, turned down his party's nomination for Governor of Florida.

1904 – Mr. Coombs became good friends with Theodore Roosevelt. While running for President, Roosevelt offered the Vice-Presidency to Coombs, but Coombs turned it down.

1905 – The Coombs House was designed and constructed by builder George Marshall. It was built with exotic lumber that Coombs had gathered from around the world.

1911 – A year of tragedy. On March 6, fire destroyed part of the house. On March 16, Mrs. Coombs died. On April 8, Mr. Coombs died. Both were buried across the street from their house in Chestnut Street Cemetery.

1911-1916 – Various family members lived in the house.

1960s – The house sat vacant and was boarded up. After years of neglect, it was vandalized and became dilapidated.

1978 – Interior designer Lynn Wilson and her husband, airline executive Bill Spohrer, discovered the house and were drawn to it. Eventually, they purchased the structure and began renovating it.

1994 – The renovations were completed, and in August the house opened for business as the Coombs House Inn. Over the years, this elegant house was featured in *Southern Living, Florida Design, Country Inns Magazine, NY Times, CNN,* and *Travel & Leisure Magazine.*

Investigation

Several of the employees and guests have had haunting experiences at the Coombs House Inn. One of the workers, Margaret, maintains that the master bedroom, known as the Coomb's Room (#8), is where most of the haunting activity seems to occur. The Raney Room (#6) and Heron Room (#7) were originally the children's bedrooms. Guests report mysterious cold spots in these rooms, and on several occasions they have heard the sound of children laughing and playing behind closed doors. However, upon inspection, the rooms have been found to be vacant.

Guests staying at the inn have not only had strange things happen in their rooms, but have also had ghostly encounters in other parts of the house. One guest was standing in the dining room gazing out the window when she recognized Mr. Coomb standing outside on the deck. She reported seeing him walk across the deck, then disappear as he walked through a solid wall.

Margaret recounted the time she was ascending the staircase and a child's helium-filled balloon inexplicably appeared out of nowhere behind her and floated past her up to the second floor where the children's bedrooms are located.

According to Margaret, a gentleman was in the attic, and in his peripheral vision he could clearly see an older woman standing next to a younger woman. As soon as he turned his head, they vanished before his eyes.

Most startling of all was the time when Margaret spied a phantom carpenter wearing a toolbelt descending the stairs, then vanishing before her eyes. It is believed he was one of the workmen involved in the renovation of the house. We were unable to determine if one of the original team of workers had indeed passed away, nor could we could we find a reason why he would choose this particular house to make his manifestation. Margaret did report that on one occasion she was cleaning the master bedroom when she was "goosed" by the ghost. Perhaps this specter is an amorous carpenter who hangs around because he's attracted to Margaret.

Gibson Inn

Location: Apalachicola, Franklin County, Florida
Address: 51 Avenue C, Apalachicola, FL 32320-2305
Phone: (850) 653-2191
Fax: (850) 653-3521
Email: info@gibsoninn.com
Website: www.gibsoninn.com
Innkeeper: Sue Bodick
Assistant Innkeeper: Sharon Soderholm

Ghost Lore

This historic Victorian inn sits on the coast overlooking Apalachicola Bay. At one time it provided room and board for weary sea-faring captains who docked nearby. Today it has a full-service bar, restaurant, and 30 guest bedrooms furnished with period antiques. With its beautiful pine and cypress carved woodwork and wrap-around verandas, people love to visit and relax "Apalach

Style," as they say. It's the perfect getaway. Some come to enjoy the "Murder Mystery Weekend," while others stay here hoping to experience a real-life ghost story.

- Some of the guest rooms, the bar, and the dining room are haunted.
- Ghosts have materialized in front of both visitors and workers.
- The feeling of being watched.
- Moving shadows and shadowy figures.
- Strange sounds. Laughter. Voices. Footsteps.
- Cold spots, especially on the third floor.
- On the third floor people can smell the sweet scent of fresh-cut roses.
- Ghosts will sometimes pull the blankets off sleeping guests.
- On the second floor witnesses have seen a little shaggy dog that vanishes.
- The piano in the bar can sometimes be heard to play on its own late at night when the bar is closed and empty.

History

1907 – The Franklin Hotel was built of heart pine and black cyprus by James Fulton "Jeff" Buck of South Carolina. He was the owner of a turpentine business.

1917 – Sisters Annie Gibson Hays and Mary Ellen "Sunshine" Gibson bought the hotel and renamed it the Gibson Inn. It was run down and didn't house a good class of people. They ran the inn with the help of Annie's son, Pat Hays and his family. Together they improved the hotel.

1925 – Annie, who was widowed, remarried and moved to

133

Tallahassee. Her son, Edward Hays, and his wife, Kathleen, helped Sunshine Gibson run the inn.

1929 to 1934 – Chapman Auditorium was built by workers from the WPA (Works Progress Administration). The workers stayed at a CCC (Civilian Conservation Corps) camp on Sumatra Road. Many of them were well-educated, college graduates, but couldn't find jobs because of the Great Depression. One of them played the piano beautifully. He had a degree in music, and would come to the Gibson Inn every Saturday night, sit down at the piano, and play for hours.

1942 – During WWII, the U.S. Army commandeered the inn as an officers' club and R&R residence for the families of military personnel waiting to be shipped out from Camp Gordon Johnston. During this time, the Hays family moved into the Buck house directly behind the hotel.

1945 – The Hays family sold the inn, and it went through a succession of owners over the years. Unable to compete with newer, more modern hotels, the inn fell into disrepair.

1977 – The state closed the inn and declared it to be a fire hazard.

1978 – A new owner opened it as a bar and pool hall.

1983 – The inn was purchased by Michael Merlo and brothers Michael and Neil Koun. They hired Tallahassee architects Rick Barnett and Dave Fronczak to restore the structure at an estimated cost of $1.2 million.

1986 – On November 1, the Gibson Inn reopened for business.

Investigation

The Minister's Wife. A minister and his wife were recently staying at the inn. The wife went downstairs to the lobby, and when she was returning to her room, she saw a luminous woman in a brown dress standing at the top of the stairs crying surrounded by an eerie mist. The apparition was there for only a moment, then demateri- alized. The frightened guest ran to her room and gave an account of her vision to her husband. He quickly dismissed it and told her she was insane. Later, sympathetic employees assured her she was- n't crazy, but explained that what she had seen was simply one of their "permanent guests."

Room 309. As the story goes, Captain Wood had taken a fancy to Sunshine Gibson and was a regular guest at her inn. Room 309 was his room of choice so as to keep an eye on his vessel, the *SS Tarpon*, which was kept anchored in Apalachicola Bay. The sea- faring captain had returned from an ocean voyage and contracted pneumonia. Sunshine attempted to nurse him back to health, but he met his demise in room 309.

Since his death, the captain has been seen in room 309 and the adjoining rooms. Most times he's friendly with the guests who share his room. He's been known to tuck guests in at night. If they are sloppy, he likes to pick up after them while they're sleeping and

put their shoes and clothes in a neat pile next to the bed. One woman even claims she received a shoulder massage from the thoughtful captain.

But there are days when the captain is in a mischievous mood. He sometimes enjoys playing pranks on people, like tapping them on the shoulder or tickling their feet. One woman even maintains he pinched her tush. Belongings can be misplaced or completely missing. He seems to be most active while people are sleeping. Sometimes he ties their shoelaces together or pulls the blankets off the bed while they're sleeping. One couple went to bed with their suitcase open and in the morning their clothes had been removed from the suitcase and flung about the room. Blinds that are closed at night will be open in the morning. Sometimes people find that the furniture has been rearranged in the middle of the night, with the chairs facing in the opposite direction. Some guests feel unwelcome in the captain's room. There was a couple who woke with a start in the middle of the night because their entire bed was shaking violently. We were told about one woman who checked into the room and unpacked her suitcase. After making a short trip down to the lobby and returning to her room, she discovered her suitcase sitting on the floor with all her clothes neatly repacked inside. She immediately returned to the front desk and asked to be moved to a different room.

The Piano. The piano in the bar is not a player piano, yet it has been known to mysteriously play on its own. Several people have had the experience of hearing the piano play after the bar had closed and the room was empty, as if invisible fingers were striking the ivory keys.

During the Great Depression, the WPA (Works Progress Administration) built the Chapman Auditorium in Apalachicola. The workers stayed at a CCC (Civilian Conservation Corps) camp on Sumatra Road. Many of these men were well educated but just couldn't find jobs because of the economy. One of these young men had a degree in music and could play the piano beautifully.

Every Saturday night from 1929-1934, he was at the Gibson Inn playing the piano and entertaining people for hours. He has long since died, and his name is forgotten, but it's believed that his spirit still occasionally returns to the inn to do what he had loved best.

Room 308. Guests who have stayed in this room report that between the hours of midnight and 3:00 a.m., they can distinctly hear the sound of high-heels walking across the floor and what sounds like furniture being moved across the room. Our investigation found that there is no attic above that room. It's what's known as a "widow's walk," a platform atop the roof that was used by the wives of captains as a lookout for incoming ships. Often these captains were lost at sea. Could it be that the lonely spirits of these women still climb to the widow's walk and eternally wait for husband who will never return?

Phantom Animals. Ghostly house pets apparently like to roam the inn. Guests have seen three phantom cats that vanish before their eyes. One, a black and white tabby, has been seen on the front desk, sleeping in the lounge, and running around the hotel. On the second floor there have been reports of a phantom canine, a shaggy little dog, who seems lively and ordinary enough, until he dissolves into thin air. When startled guests report the stray animals to the staff, a search of the premises turns up nothing. It is speculated that these were the deceased pets of the Hays family.

Room 315. The story is that a Captain Woolsy died in this room. People who have seen his apparition describe him as a short man wearing a jacket and dark blue pants. Apparently he doesn't like having his room cleaned. The cleaning staff often discover he's messed up the room minutes after they finished cleaning it. Tidy guests who stay in the room report finding their neatly-folded clothes in disarray. Another idiosyncrasy of his is that he doesn't like to stay up late. One evening, a young couple was sitting in bed reading books. At precisely midnight, both lamps on their night tables shut off. The perplexed couple turned the lights back on and continued to read. Again, both lamps shut off. At this point they decided to put their books away and turn in for the night.

The Woman in Gray. On the second floor people have seen the ghost of the former owner, Sunshine Gibson, wandering the hallways. During a recent New Year's Eve, a guest who was not familiar with the inn's haunted history went to the front desk, and inquired, "Do you know you have spooks here?" She went on to describe her encounter with a peculiar woman in gray. As the two walked towards each other in the hallway, she greeted the woman in gray with a friendly, "good evening," but the preoccupied woman walked right past her as if in a hurry and without offering a response. She kept her nose in the air as if she didn't want to be bothered, then she simply vanished into thin air.

Most witnesses describe her as wearing a long gray dress, sometimes with a white apron, and with her long hair pulled back into a bun. Apparently she still feels an obligation to maintain the inn. Some have seen her walk down the stairs and inspect the bar, then walk back upstairs and disappear. The housekeepers believe she checks up on them to make sure they're going a good job. One worker told us she put cleaning products on a bed, then stepped outside for a cigarette break. When she returned, she found the clean-

ing supplies had been moved off the bed. Another cleaning lady told us she had run out of clean linen, and the linen closet was empty, but when she had returned to her cart, it had been inexplicably restocked with fresh linen.

Phantom Phone Calls. The clerk at the front desk claims to have received phone calls from the dead. On more than one occasion, late at night, the phone will ring, and the switchboard indicates that the calls are coming from vacant guest rooms. Sometimes a strange crackling sound can be heard on the phone. Trying to find a rational explanation, the clerk will unlock the rooms and inspect them, but they're always found to be vacant. Similar calls have also originated from the bar after closing hours. Again, inspections find nobody in the room.

The Traveler. Employees at the inn also talk about a dark, mysterious figure they refer to simply as "The Traveler." Workers and guests who have seen him describe him as an imposing man wearing a black top hat, black suit, and carrying a black suitcase. He never says a word to anybody, but makes his way down the hallway and disappears. The staff claimed he checked in a long time ago and "will never checkout."

Phantom Soldiers. Witnesses have seen four soldiers wearing WWII uniforms standing outside the restaurant as if waiting to go inside. The four men appear to be talking to each other and oblivious to other people. When approached, they vanish into thin air. Could these be the spirits of men who stayed at the inn was it was used as an officers' club in the '40s?

The Mystical Experience. One person walked into the bar and had the curious experience of being transported back in time to an era when the bar and tables were no longer there. The gentleman was completely sober and level-headed, and his perception was extremely lucid. After a few minutes, the perplexed man blinked his eyes and found himself back in the present time.

Orman House

Location: Apalachicola, Franklin County, Florida
Address: The Historical Orman House, 177 Fifth Street, Apalachicola, FL 32320-1401
Phone: (850) 653-1209

Directions: Located in Apalachicola, off U.S. 98 in the downtown historical section. From Panama City, take U.S. 98 East to Apalachicola. At the stop light in Apalachicola, turn left and follow signs to the Orman House.

Ghost Lore

This antebellum home sits majestically on a bluff overlooking the Apalachicola River. It was once the home of Apalachicola merchant Thomas Orman and his wife Sarah. Today it is the home of a number of restless spirits.

- Doors knobs shake and rattle. Doors open on their own.

- Strange noises are heard upstairs.

- Mysterious scent of gunpowder in house.

- Apparitions of a woman at the top of the stairs.

- Phantom soldiers in the yard.

- A ghost on the rooftop.

History

1799 – Thomas Orman was born.

1817 – Six-foot seven-inch Orman moved from Salina, New York to New Orleans where he worked as a sugar trader. Later he moved to St. Andrews, Florida, then to Webville, Florida. He met and married his wife, Sarah Love Trippe, in Webville.

1830 – Their only child, William Thomas Orman, was born in Webville.

1834 – Thomas and Sarah moved from Webville to Apalachicola.

1836 to 38 – Thomas built the two-story house for his family. It was also used for business and social gatherings. The wood for the house was cut near Syracuse, New York and transported by ship around the Florida Keys to the bay of the Apalachicola River.

1840s to 1870s – Thomas Orman worked as a cotton merchant in Apalachicola.

1861 to 1865 – During the Civil War, their son William served as a lieutenant in the Confederate Army.

1862 – Apalachicola was captured by the Union.

1866 – William met Anna V. Smith of Mt. Pleasant. On May 30,

William and Anna were wed. They had one child, Sara.

1880 – Thomas Orman died.

1888 – William T. Orman died. The house stayed in the Orman family.

1895 – An addition was constructed on the back of the house.

1994 – The deteriorating house was purchased by Douglas and Anna Gaidy. They restored it and turned it into a bed and breakfast known as Magnolia Hall, due to the fact that Thomas Orman enjoyed magnolias. He had planted a magnolia tree in the yard and there are carved magnolia decorations in the woodwork above the doors and windows.

1999 – The house was purchased by the state of Florida and is now open as a museum.

Investigation

Legend of the Nail Keg. There is a well-known oral tradition that during the Civil War, Sarah Orman would climb onto her rooftop and place a large keg of nails on the widow's walk to create the appearance that she was doing roof repair. In actuality this was a signal to warn the townspeople whenever Union troops were in town. It was also done to warn any Confederate soldiers who might be in Apalachicola on furlough.

Some of the haunting activity seems to be related to this event. Neighbors have seen ghosts of Confederate soldiers in gray uniforms standing guard outside the house. Could these be the spirits of soldiers showing their gratitude to Sarah? Others have seen apparitions of a woman on the widow's walk and occasionally they will even see a wooden nail keg sitting up there.

Legend of Al Capone. According to persistent rumors, Al Capone had a mistress who was living in the Orman House in the

1930s, and one day she mysteriously disappeared. Some believed Capone had relocated her to a different hiding place, but others maintain she was murdered by the notorious criminal. We were able to verify that on April 2, 1930, a mysterious stranger was seen dining at a cafe in Apalachicola. The proprietor of the restaurant noticed the man bore a striking resemblance to pictures he had seen of Capone in the newspaper, so he got up the gumption to flat out ask the man if he was. To his surprise, the stranger forthrightly admitted he was indeed "Scarface Al" Capone.

Many paranormal investigators are convinced that Capone did murder his mistress and perhaps bury her body on the Orman property. Some think the apparition of a woman seen in the house might be the dead woman. One team, Forgotten Coast Paranormal Investigators, did record EVP in the house that sounded like whispers, a gun shot, and what sounded like somebody saying, "I love you."

We were told that when the house was being repainted, the wife of the painter was standing in one of the rooms. She saw a woman in white walk down the hall and enter one of the rooms. Upon inspection, the room was found to be completely empty.

Sometimes this ghost can be aggressive. When a burly man who didn't believe in ghosts attempted to climb the staircase, some unseen force pushed him back down the stairs. The terrified man quickly exited the house.

On a separate occasion, a Jehovah's Witness attempted an exorcism in the Orman House. What he experienced during the ritual is unknown. What we do know is that he, too, went running out of house and never returned.

Cobb Cemetery

Location: Baker, Okaloosa County, Florida
Address: Cobb Street, Baker, FL 32531

Directions: From Crestview go west on Hwy. 90 towards Milligan. Turn right on Old River Road. Follow Old River Road for 4.7 miles. Turn left at Cobb St. Follow the road approximately 200 yards and the cemetery is on the left.

Ghost Lore

In Okaloosa County, legends are told of "Old Man Cobb," a forlorn Civil War ghost who tirelessly wanders the cemetery late at night in search of his dead wife. Some say he will, however, happily take a breather to imbibe on the free brewskies left for him by visitors.

- The cemetery is haunted by the ghost of "Old Man Cobb" who wanders the grounds in search of his dead or missing wife. He is usually described as a gentleman of about 80 years of age wearing a Confederate Civil War uniform. The apparition is most commonly seen during the month of February, and it's said he makes his initial appearance at precisely 1:24 a.m.

- If you leave an open can of beer near the old oak tree, you will later find it mysteriously emptied.

- Another version is that when an unopened can of beer is placed near a certain headstone, after about 15 minutes it will be found empty and still closed.

- There have been sightings of hooded, phantom Ku Klux Klan members and apparitions of their lynched victims.

- People experience a feeling of trepidation as soon as they pass through the gates of the cemetery.

- Some have heard strange sounds and hushed whispers.

- Many report mysterious lights and white flashes, like the blurred motion of a sheet moving from tombstone to tombstone that inexplicably appears and then vanishes.

History

1613 – Joseph O. Cobb (1588-1654) immigrated from England to the colony of Virginia. For over a century his descendants lived in Virginia, then some moved to North Carolina, then Georgia, and finally to Florida.

1830 – July 27. One of those descendants, James M. Cobb, the son of Athal Seaborn Cobb and Martha (nee McMellon) Cobb was born in Santa Rosa County, Florida.

1853 – James married Susan Ann Peaden in Alabama.

1855 – James and Susan moved to Florida where they went on to raise eight children.

1861 – The American Civil War began.

1862 – July 15. In Santa Rosa County, James (age 32), and later his younger brothers Francis "Frank" Maine Cobb (age 26) and (Stephen) Riley Cobb (age 24) enlisted in the 15th Confederate Calvary and served under the command of Col. Henry Maury. Their regiment was organized at Mobile in the spring of 1864, and in the fall it moved into Louisiana where it played a role in the fight at Tunica. In 1863, they engaged Union troops encamped on a plantation at Tunica Bayou, Louisiana. Maury's troops attacked and routed them, killing between 50 and 60 and capturing about 25 men. The Fifteenth also made head against A. J. Smith's army.

1865 – After the War Between the States ended and his regiment disbanded, James returned home to his family and received a Florida pension.

1876 – The Cobb family purchased land in Okaloosa County and the Cobb Cemetery was established with the burial of one of James' grandaughters.

1908 – February 5. James' wife Susan died at the age of 74 and was buried in the Cobb Cemetery.

1910 – December 8. James died at the age of 80 and was buried near his wife.

1997 – The cemetery was vandalized.

Investigation

When we initially heard the stories about the cemetery, nobody could tell us which of the Cobbs buried there was supposed to be Old Man Cobb. After extensive genealogical research, we determined his identity to be James M. Cobb. He was the patriarch of the family who moved to Okaloosa County in the mid 1800s and raised a family of eight children:

146

Martha Ann Cobb (b. 1854)
Alonzo Cobb (b. 1855)
Caroline A. Cobb (b. 1858)
James B. Cobb (b. 1860)
Susan L. Cobb (b. 1862)
Sarah Elizabeth Cobb (b. 1863)
Annie Elizabeth Cobb (b. 1868)
Walter C. Cobb (b. 1871)

The Cobb family cemetery contains the graves of James M. and his wife Susan, surrounded by the graves of some of their children and several of their descendants.

Mr. Cobb was a Civil War veteran who died at the age of 80, and this certainly matches the description of the apparition. We know his wife had proceeded him in death. She died in February, which might explain why the bereaved spirit of Mr. Cobb is most often seen during that month. Although we have been unable to confirm it, we've been told Mrs. Cobb died on the morning of February 5th at precisely 1:24 a.m.

It's not known if Mr. Cobb had a propensity to drink during life that would explain his enjoyment of the barley pop in the afterlife, but that's certainly a possibility.

The Dare. If you enter the cemetery at 1:24 a.m. in February, the ghost of "Old Man Cobb" will appear to you.

Warning. The cemetery has had problems with vandalism and is regularly patrolled by the authorities. Please be respectful, don't be in there after dark, don't cause damage, and don't leave behind beer cans—empty or full.

Jameson Inn

Location: Crestview, Okaloosa County, Florida
Address: Jameson Inn of Crestview,
151 Cracker Barrel Drive, Crestview, FL 32536-2230
Phone: (850) 683-1778
Fax: (850) 683-1779
Email: crestview.fl@jamesoninns.com
Website: www.jamesoninns.com

Ghost Lore

"Hey, it's FRED!" No, we're not talking about Fred Figglehorn, the YouTube sensation with the high-pitched voice portrayed by Lucas Cruikshank. This Fred is the cigar-smoking ghost who apparently checked into the Jameson Inn, but refuses to check out. If you encounter this Fred, you might be the one screaming with a high-pitched voice.

- Strange noises are heard late at night. Sounds of doors slamming and things going bump.

- The electronic sliding doors in the lobby will sometimes open on their own.

- The elevators will sometimes be activated on the second floor and come down to the first floor, but the elevator will be empty. Security camera on the second floor reveal that nobody pushed the button.

- Rooms 208 and 206 are haunted by a ghost named "Fred."

- The smell of cigar smoke in the lobby and rooms 206 and 208.

- Cold spots.

- The little plastic door on the air conditioner in the room will sometimes open on its own.

- Guests have been awakened when the bedding was pulled off the bed by unseen hands.

History

1915 – Okaloosa County was established by the State Legislature.

1916 – Crestview was officially incorporated.

1917 – Crestview became the county seat.

2000 – Jameson Inn in Crestview was built and opened for business in April.

Investigation

The haunting activity happened soon after the inn opened. Employees working the graveyard shift began hearing strange noises: voices, knocking, doors slamming. Often the elevator would arrive at the first floor lobby, but when the doors opened, they revealed an empty elevator. A button has to be pushed to activate the elevator and that produces a chiming sound in the lobby. The staff would hear the chime, but when they checked the monitor for the surveillance camera, they didn't see anybody activate the elevator. The hallway was empty. They contacted the Otis Elevator Company in Connecticut about the problem and were told that what is happening really isn't possible. Then the electric sliding doors in the lobby began opening on their own when nobody was walking through—at least, nobody visible. It was at this point when the employees decided the place was haunted and christened their friendly ghost as "Fred."

Later, guests began to complain of ghostly activity in room 206. It was a non-smoking room, yet they would suddenly get a strong whiff of cigar smoke, then it was gone. They also encountered cold spots in parts of the room. Sometimes guests would be awaken when they felt invisible hands pulling the bedding off their bed. Others would wake up in the morning and find their luggage or clothing had been rearranged during the night. According to the front desk, the ghost has apparently changed rooms, and is now haunting room 208.

On rare occasions, guests have caught a glimpse of Fred. Sometimes they see him standing near the elevator; other times he's walking down the hallway on the second floor. They describe him as a young man in his early 20s wearing a sleeveless shirt. Sometimes he's chomping on a cigar. He's visible for a moment, then disappears. Some of the employees think they've seen his blurred image on the video camera surveillance.

We did some checking and found no evidence that anybody had ever died in the hotel. Nor was anybody killed during the construction of it. We considered the possibility that someone died in a house that was built on that site sometime in the past, but it turned out the Jameson Inn was built on an empty lot that had never been previously built on. The employees told us there were long-time rumors that the forest behind the inn was haunted, so perhaps there is a connection there.

1872 John Denham House Bed & Breakfast

Location: Monticello, Jefferson County, Florida
AKA: The Denham/Lacy House, The Virginia C. Turnbull House
Address: 555 West Palmer Mill Road, Monticello, Florida 32344-1360
Phone: (850) 997-4568 or (850) 933-8104
Email: pat@johndenhamhouse.com
Website: www.johndenhamhouse.com
Innkeeper: Pat Inmon

Ghost Lore

ABC News designated Monticello as "The South's Most Haunted Small Town." According to Big Bend Ghost Trackers, one in three homes in the town has ghosts. If a person is skeptical, they suggest spending the night in the John Denham House will quickly make a believer out of them. In fact, *USA Today* listed this bed and breakfast as the "second best place to sleep with a ghost." Surprisingly, a lot of guests do want to sleep with a ghost and request the "haunted room" when they make their reservation.

- The Blue Room is haunted.

- The apparition of a ghost known as "Aunt Sarah" walks the hallways.

- The spirit of a Union soldier haunts the property.

- Guests wake up in the middle of the night for no reason.

- Cold spots.

- The sound of voices and footsteps.

- Cell phone and camera batteries will drain.

- Alarm clocks in all the rooms will go off at the same time in the afternoon.

- Lights flicker and turn on and off on their own.

- The feeling of being watched and not being alone.

History

1872 – The house was built by John Denham. Over the years it has had several owners including John Denham, Mrs. O. Lacy, Virginia C. Turnbull, the Andersons, the Williams, the Sullivans, and the current owner Patricia Hays Inmon.

1982 – It was added to the National Register of Historic Places.

Investigation

Contrary to rumors, John Denham was not a captain and his ghost has not been seen in the cupola of the house. According to tradition, the house was built in 1872, but might actually date as far back to 1850.

Scottish immigrant John Denham (1856-1908) built the house and lived there with his wife Adair (nee Scott) Denham (1864-1924). Together they raised five sons. Other long-time residents included Virginia C. Turnbull (1869-1939) and Mrs. O. Lacy who was the third owner and her family had three generations in the house.

Aunt Sarah. At some point a woman known as "Aunt Sarah" lived in the house with her brother. Sarah loved children and was engaged to be married, but for unknown reasons the wedding never happened, and she died childless. Today she haunts the Blue Room. Whenever a new mother and her infant stay there, Aunt Sarah switches on the lights. Perhaps it's out of jealousy. Other times she's been known to tuck guests in at night.

Haunting Activity. Sometimes up to five alarm clocks in separate rooms will go off during the day, usually in unison. According to the owner, this happens several times a month.

Electrical equipment like cell phones and cameras will lose their charge. Even when fresh batteries are installed, they will instantly drain.

Guests have awakened in the middle of the night for no apparent reason. Sometimes they see mysterious lights moving about the room.

People have seen full-bodied apparitions in the house. One is a man, perhaps John Denham, wearing nineteenth-century clothing; the other is a woman, perhaps Aunt Sarah, wearing a wedding dress.

Author Terry Fisk and his wife Jeannine spent the night in the house. They inexplicably woke up simultaneously at about 3:00 a.m. At that time they were unaware that other guests had had this experience. Being wide awake, they decided to get dressed, grab their investigative equipment, and explore the house. They checked out the second floor, but by the time the reached the top of the stairs to the cupola, all their batteries had died.

Big Bend Ghost Trackers. When the local Ghost Tracker group visited the house, they encountered the usual cold spots and sudden unexplained temperature drops. A couple of the team members were able to go into a trance and communicate with two of the spirits: a man and a woman. The mediums weren't certain if it was Aunt Sarah and the man she planned to marry or if it was John Denham and a mistress. Another medium made contact with a Union soldier who either died on the property or was buried there. She also made contact with a woman in the Blue Room who was most likely Aunt Sarah. The group captured EVPs and photographic anomalies and heard the unexplained sound of footsteps on the hardwood floors.

Holiday Inn SunSpree Resort

Location: Panama City Beach, Bay County, Florida
Address: 11127 West Highway 98,
Panama City Beach, FL 32407-3529
Phone: (850) 234-1111
Toll-Free: 1-888-HOLIDAY (888-465-4329)
Fax: (850) 235-1907

Ghost Lore

When most people envision a haunted location, they usually think of a dilapidated old house with crawling spiders and flying bats. Their first thought isn't of a luxurious hotel with a pool and tiki bar situated next to a white sandy beach and turquois waters. At the SunSpree Resort, not all the guests lay out in the sun; some lurk in the shadows and only come out at night.

155

- An apparition of a decapitated spring breaker appears in the room at 4:00 a.m.

- The television will turn on by itself.

- The radio alarm clock will go off when not set. The radio changes stations.

- Belongings will disappear and later reappear.

- Cold spots.

- Voices and strange sounds.

- Guests will wake up at 4:00 a.m. without explanation.

History

1953 – Panama City Beach was chartered.

1960s – Spring break started gaining popularity with American youths.

1970s – Condominiums and resorts were built on the Panama City Beach coast and the area became a popular travel destination for young people on spring break. During this decade, the fad of "balcony jumping" began.

1990 – The Holiday Inn SunSpree was constructed.

1990s – Several young people were injured or killed at the SunSpree while balcony climbing.

2001 – The hotel was renovated.

Investigation

The slogan of Panama City Beach is "The World's Most Beautiful Beaches." At one time the area was informally known as the "Redneck Riviera" because of the older houses and tumble-down motels. A construction boom in the '70s replaced those structures with luxurious hotels, and the improvement attracted hordes of spring breakers looking for warm weather and excitement. With a resident population of about 9,000, the area received close to five million visitors each year, and more hotels were built.

It was during that same decade when spring breakers saw the introduction of a popular fad known as "balcony jumping" (aka balcony climbing or balcony diving). After a few drinks, some of the revelers staying at the hotels would decide to play Spider-Man and climb from one balcony to another. Needless to say, this activity led to numerous accidents resulting in serious injuries and even death. In fact, this is the reason why Las Vegas hotels have no balconies. Although balcony climbing is now illegal under Florida state law and punishable by fine or jail time, this dangerous spring break ritual still persists.

The Holiday SunSpree Resort, with 15 floors and 340 rooms (all with private balconies), was built in 1990. Every spring it has its share of balcony accidents. There are rumors about one particular student's balcony diving escapade at the SunSpree Resort that

resulted in a grizly death. Apparently the young man was staying on one of the upper floors and attempted to climb from his balcony to the one beneath—while intoxicated. He miscalculated and fell to his death. As the story goes, he either broke his neck or was decapitated during the fall when his head struck one of the balconies below. Some believe his spirit still resides on the upper levels of the hotel. Several guests claim to have seen an apparition of the headless spring breaker standing in their room between the two double beds. They say he looks like a typical spring breaker, decked out in colorful shorts and a white tee-shirt. He wears sunglasses, but because he has no head, he wears them on a rope-cord strap around his neck. He only makes his appearance at 4:00 a.m., which is believed to have been the hour of his fatal accident.

Although he never harms the guests, he can be mischievous. For example, he likes to turn on the TV and play around with the alarm clock radio. Sometimes he will move belongings around and even hide them. Often he will wake people at precisely 4:00 a.m. It seems he just wants to make his presence known. Perhaps he's there as a warning to others that they shouldn't be foolish enough to engage in the same reckless behavior he once did.

The Dare. If you stay in a room on the top floor, the ghost of the decapitated spring breaker will appear at precisely 4:00 a.m.

The Clara Barkley Dorr House

Location: Pensacola, Escambia County, Florida
Address: The Clara Barkley Dorr House,
311 South Adams Street, Pensacola, FL 32502-6001
Phone: (850) 595-5985 Ext. 100 or (850) 595-5995
Website: www.historicpensacola.org

Ghost Lore

Clara Barkley Dorr, a wealthy widow, built this house and raised her children on her own. Both tour guides and tourists have seen spooky evidence that the deceased widow and her children have never left home.

- Feelings of discomfort.

- Shadowy figures seen in the peripheral vision.

159

- Objects get moved around.

- The alarm will go off...without power.

- Cold spots.

- The feeling of being watched.

- The scent of fresh-cut roses.

- The sound of crying in the sewing room (sick room).

- Supernatural activity on the second floor and at the top of the staircase.

- EVPs and photographic anomalies.

History

1696 – The first permanent settlement was established in this area by the Spanish. Seville Square was the center of the old settlement.

1781 to 1821 – Lots were platted in downtown Pensacola.

1825 – Clara Garnier Barkley was born. She was the daughter of shipping merchant George W. Barkley and French native Clara Louise Garnier. Her parents built their home overlooking Pensacola Bay that same year. The house is currently known as the "Barkley House."

1840 – On September 15, she married Noel Armande (or Armando) Vienne (b. 1821). He died shortly after without fathering any children.

1849 – On December 12, she married timber magnate Ebenezer Walker Dorr (b. 1823), the son of Sheriff Ebenezer Dorr IV. He was part-owner of a mill in Bagdad. Together the couple had eight children with two or more dying in infancy.

1870 – On October 14, Eben Dorr died of yellow fever. That same year, his eldest son, Hawkes Barkley Dorr, died at the age of 20. Eben's share of the mill was distributed to Clara. With the wealth she inherited, she bought land near Seville Square and built a two-story Greek Revival house, later known as the Clara Barkley Dorr House. While living here, she raised her five remaining children.

1872 – Clara and her children moved into the house.

1896 – In her senior years, Clara moved into a hotel.

1899 – Clara Garnier Barkley Vienne Dorr died at the age of 74 and was buried in St. John's Cemetery next to her husband.

1899 to 1904 – The house changed hands several times. For a short time it even served as a private school for the children of Pensacola's wealthy families.

1904 to 1954 – The house had one owner.

1965 – The Pensacola Heritage Foundation purchased the house and restored it. It is furnished with antiques from the 1850s to 1890s.

1974 – It was added to the U.S. National Register of Historic Places.

1975 – The Historic Pensacola Preservation Board purchased it.

Currently – The home is a museum known as the Clara Barkley Dorr House, and it's part of the Seville Square walking tour in Pensacola's historic district.

Investigation

In 1849, Clara Barkley married timber magnate Ebenezer Walker Dorr. He was part-owner of a mill in Bagdad. His father was note-worthy as Escambia County's first sheriff, and his great-grandfa-ther was famous for being a rider with Paul Revere during his historical ride; Dorr rode through the southwestern Boston area, taking the alarm throughout Roxbury and beyond. Together Clara and Eben had eight children with two or more dying in infancy. In 1870, Clara lost both her husband and her oldest son. After inheriting Eben's share of the mill and becoming a wealthy woman, she purchased land in Pensacola's most prestigious neighborhood and built a huge Greek Revival house where she raised her five remaining children. The family has long since passed away and the house is now a museum, but many believe Clara and her children haunt the house.

Tour guides have had artifacts and other objects mysteriously disappear. After hours of frantic searching, the objects reappear just as mysteriously. It's believed to be the playful activity of Clara's deceased children. In the sewing room, which was the family sick room in Clara's day, people have heard the sound of a young child's whimpering cries. It's believed this is the ghost of one of her children who died during the 1880s yellow fever epidemic. Often the guides will feel a tugging on their dress or pant leg, reminiscent of a small child trying to get their attention.

In the formal fitting room, tourists have caught a glimpse of Clara in the floor-to-ceiling mirror. They describe her as prim and proper, decked out in nineteenth century attire. People have also seen her in one of the rooms on the second floor. She appears as her younger self dancing about the room, and then she vanishes. Other times she's been seen on the balcony staring into the distance with a somber and contemplative expression.

The Dare. There is a floor-to-ceiling mirror in the formal sitting room. If a young woman stands before the mirror attired in a short skirt or shorts that ride up too high, she will feel the prudish ghost of Clara tugging at the hem, as if trying to make it longer.

Old Christ Church

Location: Pensacola, Escambia County, Florida
AKA: Christ Church
Address: 405 South Adams Street, Pensacola, FL 32502
Phone: (850) 595-5985

Ghost Lore

Built in 1832, Old Christ Church is the state's oldest church still standing in its original location. In the 19th century, three of its rectors—Joseph Saunders, Frederick R. Peake, and David Dubois Flower—were buried beneath the floor of the church vestry. Over the years, their unmarked graves were forgotten, until 1988 when an archeological team unearthed their bones and apparently allowed their spirits to roam free.

* Sweet scent of fresh roses.

- Apparitions of three monks.

History

1781 – Spain captured Pensacola from the British. During this time no Protestant services were allowed.

1819 – The Adams-Onis Treaty was signed between the U.S. and Spain, granting Florida to the U.S.

1821 – On July 17, General Andrew Jackson formally took control of Florida at Pensacola. Jackson lived in Pensacola and served as Territorial Governor. That same year, his wife Rachael invited Protestant missionaries to come to their city.

1827 – The General Missionary Society of the Episcopal Church sent the Rev. Ralph Williston. He spent three weeks in Pensacola to meet with citizens and plan the establishment of a Protestant church.

1830 – Construction began on the church building. The land cost $400 and the church cost $4,500.

1832 – Construction was completed.

1840 – Rev. Joseph Saunders, the 4th Rector, died of yellow fever and was buried under the vestry room of the church.

1846 – Rev. Frederick R. Peake, the 5th Rector, died and was buried next to Saunders.

1853 – Rev. David Dubois Flower, the 9th Rector, died of yellow fever and was also buried beneath the church.

1861 to 1865 – The American Civil War. Most of the church members evacuated to Alabama. Union troops seized the church building and used it as an infirmary, barracks, and jail.

1865 – After the war, Union soldiers left and the congregation returned. The church was in a state of disrepair and the graves beneath the vestry room had been disturbed.

1879 – The congregation spent $5,000 to repair and restore the building.

1903 – The last church service was held in Old Christ Church.

1936 – Old Christ Church was deconsecrated and deeded to the city. It became Pensacola's first public library. Later it housed the Pensacola Historical Society's museum.

1974 – The church was listed with the U.S. National Register of Historic Places.

1988 – An archaeological dig discovered the bodies of Saunders, Peake, and Flower.

1996 – The title for the building was transferred from the city back to the church.

1999 – After spending nearly one million dollars to restore the building, the church transferred ownership back to the city.

2004 – The building sustained damage during Hurricane Ivan.

Investigation

Old Christ Church was built in 1832. In the 1840s and '50s, three of the rectors were buried in the church beneath the floor of the vestry room. Years later, the vestry room was torn down, and the church building was extended 20 feet over that area and covered the unmarked graves. The three rectors and their graves were eventually forgotten.

In 1988, Rev. Beverly Madison Currin, the 15th rector, invited Judith Bense of the Archaeological Institute of the University of West Florida to conduct an archeological dig at Old Christ Church. After a two month search for artifacts, the student archaeologists located three decomposing coffins and exhumed the graves of the three priests.

The team stored the bones and their equipment in the nearby Lear-Rocheblave House because it had an electronic alarm system. The bones were placed in three individual coffin-like boxes, and neatly laid out in their correct anatomical positions. Other artifacts were also kept there, along with their tools, cameras, and other equipment. That night, the alarm was set and the doors were locked. The following morning, the archaeologists returned to the building. After unlocking the door and shutting off the alarm, they went to retrieve their equipment and discovered the bones in each individual coffin had been moved. They were rearranged and scattered about almost as if somebody had picked up the boxes and shook them like dice in a Yahtzee cup. Small bone fragments were also found on the floor. The students joked that it looked like the skeletons climbed out of the coffins in the middle of the night and danced about the room. Since that day, the unmistakable scent of roses has been detected in Lear-Rocheblave House—though there are no rosebushes in the area.

A local carpenter was hired to build new identical coffins for the three rectors. He was doing the work in his garage late at night with the garage door open. He looked out and saw three priests standing on the edge of the darkness talking to each other. When he walked out to greet them, they vanished before his eyes.

A ceremony was held for the reinterment of the bones beneath the church floor. Attending the services was Gary Powell, a paraplegic student from the University of West Florida. As he watched the procession, he noticed three barefooted priests wearing dark robes and stoles around their shoulders. The one in the center had a somber expression and was carrying a large black leather-covered book embossed with a gold leaf cross. The two on his sides seemed more jovial and were engaged in a conversation. Powell looked away, but when he looked back, they had vanished. He asked the people next to him if they knew where the three men went, but nobody else had seen them. Later he learned from a priest that the rectors were traditionally buried with bare feet. Their burial clothes consisted of robes with stoles and they were buried with a black prayer book. Since Powell's sighting, people have noticed the scent of roses in Old Christ Church.

Allison House

Location: Quincy, Gadsden County, Florida
Address: 215 North Madison Street, Quincy, FL 32351-2444
Phone: (850) 875-2511
Toll-Free: 1-888-904-2511
Fax: (850) 875-2511
Email: innkeeper@tds.net
Website: www.allisonhouseinn.com
Innkeepers: Stuart and Eileen Johnson

Ghost Lore

This historic bed and breakfast prides itself on being close to area
attractions, both in Quincy and northern Florida. One of those
attractions happens to be ghosts.

- The ghost of former governor A. K. Allison still resides in the
  house he built.

- Sarah Harris, the governor's daughter, haunts the house she used to live in.

- Cold spots and temperature changes have been sensed.

- Footsteps have been heard.

History

1810 – On December 10th, Abraham Kurkindolle Allison was born in Jones County, Georgia. He was the son of Capt. James and Sarah (nee Fannin) Allison.

1830s – Allison was a general commanding the Wars of Indian Removal.

1832 – He moved to Apalachicola and became their first mayor.

1843 – General Allison moved to Quincy and built a house there. It originally sat on the corner of King and Madison.

1852 – Allison was Speaker of the Florida House.

1865 – A. K. Allison became the president of the Florida Senate. On April 1, he became the sixth governor of the state of Florida after Gov. John Milton committed suicide. As governor, he signed the peace treaty with the Union, ending Florida's role in the Civil War. In June, he was arrested by federal authorities and imprisoned for several months.

1867 – A. K. Allison and his second wife, Elizabeth Susan Coleman, had a daughter, Sarah Fannin Allison, who was born in this house. Years later, Sarah married Ross Gilliam Harris in the same house.

1893 – A. K. Allison died on July 8 in Quincy at the age of 82.

1895 – His wife Elizabeth died. Sarah, being the youngest child, inherited the house.

1925 – Sarah had the house moved to its present location. It was raised up on tall brick piling and the lower portion was enclosed to create a boarding house on the upper floor, which she and her husband Ross operated. The couple continued to live in the downstairs. Their bedroom was the room now known as The Country Room.

1940s to 1950s - After Sarah and Ross passed away, the upstairs was rented out as apartments and the lobby was used as a credit bureau. The owner lived downstairs.

1990 – The house was converted into a bed and breakfast—the first in Quincy.

1996 – Stuart and Eileen Johnson purchased it.

2002 – The Big Bend Ghost Trackers conducted an investigation at the Allison House.

Investigation

According to innkeepers Stuart and Eileen Johnson, the most active areas in the house are The Governor's Room, The Garden Room, the upstairs hallway, and the staircase. Stuart also works at the haunted Quincy Music Theatre and Eileen is employed by the American Institute of Architecture. They explained that The Hunt Room was originally the governor's master bedroom. The Governor's Room and The Allison Room used to be parlors.

Often guests who stay there with children find their children to be intuitively aware of the ghosts. One young girl, about nine years old, kept asking about the spirits she could see.

The Garden Room. Some people report having an uneasy feeling staying in this room. This was Sarah's bedroom when she was a child. One guest encountered a ghostly woman dressed in white on two separate occasions. The first time the woman was sitting in a chair and the second time she was sitting on the end of the bed.

Big Bend Ghost Trackers. The Johnsons talked about an investigation conducted there by The Big Bend Ghost Trackers. Two of the Ghost Trackers were intuitives who were able to contact a spirit in The Garden Room. It was the spirit of a young woman who identified herself as Sarah. They determined she was "the woman in white" that others had seen. They were also able to communicate with two male entities. One identified himself as Anderson, and the name of the other gentleman sounded like "Greenfield." At the time of the investigation, the intuitives were not aware that the governor's daughter was named Sarah. Further research by the team later uncovered an 1890 census that listed five Anderson families who lived in the neighborhood. They also learned the Allisons had an extended family member named "Granville," which sounds similar to Greenfield.

The psychics also encountered the governor himself in the upstairs hallway and near the staircase. They could even hear his footsteps as he walked down the hall. Later they could sense him in the backyard searching for his wife.

After setting up their equipment, the Ghost Tracker team captured moving orbs on night vision video cameras. They also videotaped what appeared to be a "ribbon of smoke" that floated up the staircase and down the hallway. Later, digital thermometers recorded a sudden temperature drop. Within seconds after that, EMF readings spiked.

The spiritual contact and instrument recording convinced the team that the Allison House was inhabited by Governor Allison and his daughter Sarah. The Johnsons even had a document from the team certifying the bed and breakfast as an authentic haunted house.

Leaf Theatre

Location: Quincy, Gadsden County, Florida
Address: 118 East Washington Street,
Quincy, FL 32351-2415
Phone: (850) 875-9444
Email: qmt@qmtonline.com
Website: www.qmtonline.com

Ghost Lore

The Leaf Theatre was named for the tobacco leaf, which at one time was an important part of the area's economy. For many decades, people attended the theatre to watch movies and in more recent years to see live performances. During the last twenty years strange things have occurred in the theatre. Some say the building is haunted by several spirits, including a former projectionist and a woman who worked in the concession stand. In fact, after a thorough investigation by paranormal researchers, the theatre was awarded a plaque to certify it as an authenticated haunted location.

- Cold spots.

- Doors slam shut on their own.

- Objects get moved around.

- Lights turn on.

- Hair stands up on neck.

- The sound of footsteps.

- The feeling of being watched.

- Strange noises and the sound of moving objects.

- Voices have been heard. People have heard their name called out.

- Shadowy figures have been seen in the balcony.

- Apparitions of a man, a woman, a girl, and a boy. They've been seen backstage, in the balcony, and in the auditorium.

History

1949 – The Leaf Theatre was built. It originally had a seating capacity of 1,200. Its namesake was the shade tobacco leaf that was grown in the area and used for cigar wrappers.

1960s – Single-screen theatres were being squeezed out by the multiplex cinemas.

1980 – The Leaf Theatre closed down, and the building sat empty for several years.

1981 – Sherrille Odel McDaniel, who worked as the projectionist at the Leaf Theatre for over 20 years, passed away at the age of 70.

1983 – The theatre was purchased and renovated through private donations and grants. It was incorporated as The Quincy Music

173

Theatre and reopened that year hosting Broadway plays and other musical productions.

Investigation

There are at least four ghosts who haunt the theatre. Several people have seen these spirits, and their descriptions have been remarkably similar, and the sightings seem to consistently occur in the same locations.

The Man. An apparition of a man wearing khaki pants has been seen on and off for nearly twenty years. He's been seen by several of the actors and even the cleaning lady. He's been sighted in the balcony, in the projection room, and walking around the building. But most often he's seen in the in the auditorium, in the front row of the center section, sitting in the third seat from the right (as viewed from the stage). When all the seats are folded in the up position, this particular one is always found in the down position.

The Woman. People have also seen an apparition of an older woman. She's been described as "prim and proper" older lady with her hair styled in a bun and dressed in 1950's style clothing. Witnesses have seen her sitting in the back row of the right section, in the first seat on the right (as viewed from the stage). Some witnesses have recognized her as a former employee who used to work in the concession stand during the decades of the 1950s and '60s. In life, she would sit in that area near the lobby door, so she could quickly exit the theatre when she saw a patron leaving to purchase a drink or snack.

The Girl. A young girl has been seen standing in the left aisle. The only description we've heard is that she's wearing a dress. A manager was working in the theatre late one night. He was standing on a ladder adjusting the stage lights, when he noticed a little girl in the auditorium, standing in the third row. She was quietly watching him as he worked. His first thought was that a child had accidentally gotten locked in the building with him. He asked her what she was doing there, and started climbing down the ladder, but by the time turned around she had disappeared. He searched the building high and low for over an hour, but it was empty and all the doors were locked.

The Boy. The young boy is seen less frequently, but when he does appear, he's been seen in the front row of the left section, sitting in the last seat to the left.

When we spoke with the manager of the theatre, Bill Mock, he described a ghostly encounter he had late one night while building sets on the stage. It was about 2:00 a.m., and he had sat down his cordless power drill and turned away for just a moment. When he turned back, the drill was gone. He found it over four feet from where he had originally laid it. He had a feeling somebody else might be in the theatre, so he turned on all the lights and searched every room, but the building was empty.

According to Bill, a number of strange things have happened in the theatre. There have been times when he shut off all the lights and locked up the building for the night, only to return in the morning and find all the lights turned on. Often performers will be on stage rehearsing when they look out and see the apparitions sitting in the auditorium. People have heard their name called out, but nobody was there. A number of people have reported strange experiences on the landing for the stairs that lead up to the balcony. A mysterious cold spot lingers in that area; sometimes it's 20 degrees colder than the rest of the theatre. People who walk through there experience strange sensations. According to a cleaning lady, she was vacuuming the landing when she felt some type of supernatural energy pass through her body. She went running from the theatre.

The Big Bend Ghost Trackers. In 2006, the Big Bend Ghost Trackers, based out of Monticello, traveled to Quincy and conducted a formal investigation of the theatre. Founder and director Betty Davis brought in her team, and they set up their high-tech equipment. Being a sensitive, Davis sat in the darkened theatre and meditated, in an attempt to channel any spirits who might be present. A few minutes later, she succeeded in communicating with a spirit who appeared to her as a short, stocky man wearing khaki pants with a brown leather belt. She said he was a balding man with light brown hair, and he kept checking his wristwatch as if he were on a fixed schedule. She also picked up on the name "Gibson." Later, another team member, Lacey White, channeled the name "Charlie."

Afterwards the team met with the theatre manager and a couple of newspaper reporters to share the information they had channeled. The manager said the description of the man matched that of a former projectionist who passed away several years ago. The names "Charlie" and "Gibson" had no significance that he was aware of.

Two weeks later, after the investigation had been written up in the *Gadsden County News* and *Havana News Herald*, Betty Davis was contacted by Charles McDaniel from Chattahoochee. He had read the newspaper articles and immediately recognized her description of the spirit as being his late father, Sherrille Odel McDaniel, who worked as the projectionist at the Leaf Theatre for over twenty years. He said people knew his father as "Mac," and when he worked at the theatre, he was known for obsessively checking his watch because it was his responsibility to make sure the movies began on schedule. He also had to clear the theatre after the show so the next group could come in to be seated.

What about the names "Charlie" and "Gibson"? As a young boy, McDaniel would visit his father at work, and his father called him "Charlie." "Gibson," he explained, was the name of the theatre in Chattahoochee where his father worked as a projectionist prior to taking the job in Quincy.

Knott House Museum

Location: Tallahassee, Leon County, Florida
Address: Knott House Museum, 301 East Park Avenue, Tallahassee, FL 32301-1513
Phone: (850) 922-2459
Website: www.flheritage.com

Ghost Lore

It's known as "The House That Rhymes." William Knott's wife used to write short poems on slips of paper and tie them to the furniture with satin ribbons. Luella Knott died eight days after her husband's death, and some believe she may have had a premonition of her own impending demise when she penned the following poem shortly after his passing.

> The light grows dimmer every day,
> My voice grows weaker when I pray,

177

Since then;
Not that I'd want to call him back, ah, no!
God knows I wanted him to go,
But somehow something hurts me so,
Since then.
There's nothing now to hold me here,
And everything to draw me there,
Since then;
Sweet sorrows taught me how to see
And hear and feel, and want to be
With that dear voice that's calling me -
Since then.

Did she hear her late husband summoning her from the great beyond? Does her spirit still roam the floors of the house, trailing a whiff of perfume in her wake? Has their son made his ghostly presence known in a photograph taken in the study?

- Haunted by the ghost of Charlie Knott.
- The sound of footsteps on the second floor.
- Cold spots.
- The scent of floral perfume.

History

1843 – Built by free black builder George Proctor. Attorney Thomas Hagner and his wife Catherine Gamble lived there.

1845 – Thomas died in the house. Catherine converted the residence into a boarding house.

1857 – Catherine moved out and went to live with her mother.

1865 – The house served as temporary Union Headquarters. On May 20th, Brigadier General Edward M. McCook read the Emancipation Proclamation from the front porch to announce the end of the Civil War and freedom of the slaves.

1883 – Dr. George Betton bought the house from Catherine and made it his home and office. Betton assisted in the early medical training of his carriage driver, William J. Gunn, who became Florida's first black physician.

1896 – Dr. Betton died in the house.

1919 – Dr. John W. Scott and his wife Caroline acquired the house.

1920 – Dr. Scott died in the house.

1928 – William Valentine Knott and Luella Pugh Knott purchased the house. Mr. Knott was the state treasurer. Mrs. Knott was a poet. They had three children.

1965 – Mr. Knott died at the age of 101. Mrs. Knott died eight days

Photo of ghost in the library.

later at the age of 93. Their son, J. Charles "Charlie" Knott, inherited the house and continued to live there.

1985 – Charlie died in the house, and the Historic Tallahassee Preservation Board became the beneficiary.

1992 – After extensive renovations, the Knott House Museum opened to the public.

1997 – Its administration was transferred to the Museum of Florida History.

Investigation

When a group of psychics visited the house, one sensed the presence of a young boy who had a physical problem which prevented him from being able to climb the stairs. Subsequent research by the museum's staff revealed there was a boy with polio who had lived in the house at one time.

Several visitors to the museum have reported the strong scent of a woman's floral perfume that suddenly fills the room and is gone a moment later. According to the staff, Luella Knott was known to wear such a fragrance.

Employees at the museum working after-hours will often hear the sounds of footsteps and movement on the second floor. The sound of shoes walking on the wooden floors is unmistakable. When they go upstairs to investigate, they are perplexed to find all the rooms to be empty.

The most amazing piece of evidence is a photograph of the study taken during the restoration of the house. When the photo was taken, the library was empty. But when the picture was developed, it showed the blurred image of a man sitting in a chair near the bookcase. Some of the staff members believe it to be the ghost of Charlie Knott. The museum has put the photo on display for visiting tourists. Be sure to ask to see it.

Velda Mound Park

Location: Tallahassee, Leon County, Florida
Address: Arbor Hill, Killearn Estates, Tallahassee, FL 32309

Directions: From Thomasville Road (Hwy. 61/319) go east on Killarney Way. Turn right on Raymond Diehl Road. Turn left on Vassar Road. Turn right on Baldwin Drive West and follow it as it curves to the left and becomes Baldwin Drive South. Just after passing Mound Drive on your left, Velda Mound Park is on your right.

Ghost Lore

The premier Arbor Hill neighborhood within the sub-division of Killearn Estates in Tallahassee is not the kind of place where you would expect to find an Indian mound. Nor is it the kind of place where you would expect to encounter a phantom wolf, but many in this neighborhood have learned to expect the unexpected.

- Apparitions of Native Americans have been seen.

- A phantom white wolf can be seen glowing and heard howling late at night.

History

1450 to 1625 C.E. – The Apalachee Indians lived in this area. The home for a village leader was probably built on this mound, while the rest of the tribe lived on the land surrounding the mound. They built dwellings and planted fields and gardens. The mound most likely also served as their town hall.

c. 1565 – When the Spanish arrived, the site had been abandoned probably because most of the trees had been cut down and the land was no longer fertile.

1704 – British soldiers attacked the Apalachee Indians and drove most of them out of the Tallahassee area. European settlers used the land for farming.

1940s – This land and the mound were owned by the Velda Dairy Farm.

1950s – The mound was damaged when someone bulldozed a trench through the middle of it.

1964 – Land developer J. T. Williams and his partners, Mallory Horne and Bill Cartee, drafted plans to turn 3,800 acres of the Velda Dairy Farm into the county's largest subdivisions.

1969 – An archaeological dig at the mound found the remains of three circular homes, storage pits, pottery, and other artifacts.

1973 – The Velda Dairy property began to be developed into a housing complex known as Arbor Hill. Over the next decade, three developers sequentially owned the property. The surrounding land experienced residential development, and the site of the mound became an unauthorized trash dump. It was also subjected to vandalism, digging, and looting.

1982 – Land developers donated a 1.91-acre parcel containing the mound to the State of Florida.

1999 – The Bureau of Archaeological Research filled in the trench that had been bulldozed through the mound and began work to establish the Velda Mound Park.

2006 – About 10 volunteers from the Panhandle Archaeological Society at Tallahassee (P.A.S.T.) collaborated with Public Lands Archaeology to clean up the Velda Mound Park. Their efforts have preserved the historical landmark.

Currently – P.A.S.T. is in charge of the stewardship and care of the mound.

Investigation

The Velda Mound Park was once an Indian village. Several people who have visited the park after dark have seen apparitions of a group of Indians huddled around a glowing campfire. After a minute or two, the fire fades and the vision vanishes.

Other after-dark visitors report seeing a large, white wolf that radiantly glows in the dark. They've seen it circle the mound then disappear. Late at night, many people living in the neighborhood have heard the blood-curdling sound of the howling of a wolf—especially during a full moon. In Native American traditions, the wolf is said to be a "teacher." For thousands of years, humans have followed the wolves and learned from their methods of hunting and from their social structure.

The mound has suffered years of abuse, being vandalized, looted, trashed, and dug into. It's only recently that people have restored it and learned to respect it. Perhaps Wolf the Teacher and the original residents have returned to express their gratitude.

SOUTHEAST FLORIDA

Historic Smallwood's Store

Location: Chokoloskee, Collier County, Florida
Physical Address: 360 Mamie Street, Chokoloskee, Florida 34138
Mailing Address: P.O. Box 367, Chokoloskee, Florida 34138
Phone: (239) 695-2989
Fax: (239) 695-4454
Website: www.florida-everglades.com/chokol/smallw.htm

Directions: From Everglades City head toward Chokoloskee Island (3 miles). Once on the island turn right on Chokoloskee Dr. Turn left on Mamie St. and the museum will be straight back on the dead end road.

Ghost Lore

Many years ago, a local farmer came up with a sinister plan to help cut costs on his farm. Each season the farmer would hire a group of migrant workers to help tend to his fields. The farmer decided that at the end of the season, when the time came to pay the men for their work, he would simply murder them and dump their mutilated bodies in the dense waters of the swamp. His devious plan played out for several years until the townsfolk started to notice all the missing workers that never seemed to return from his farm. Horrified by what had taken place at the farm, the townsfolk took matters into their own hands, and the farmer soon joined his workers in death.

- The spirit of the slain killer continues to wander his death site.

- Visitors to the area often are overcome with a horrible sense of dread.

History

1855 – Edgar Watson was born.

1906 – Ted Smallwood, a local businessman, opened a small remote trading post with his wife, Mamie, that dealt in fruits and vegetables, furs and hides, and other necessities of the time.
1910 – On October 24th Edgar Watson, the alleged murderer, came into town for supplies when he was gunned down by a group of locals on the docks of Smallwood's Store.

1916 – The store was rebuilt near the water's shore after a hurricane swept through the town.

1974 – The trading post was placed on the National Register of Historic Places.

1982 – The store closed down. Over 90 percent of the items the store contained were left inside boarded up.

1989-90 – Ted's granddaughter, Lynn McMillin, began the long process of renovating the store in order to open it as a museum and gift shop.

1992 – Smallwood's Store was re-opened to the public.

Currently – The museum is open to the public and is providing visitors with a chance to explore the fascinating history of the area.

Investigation

The store is also known as the Smallwood's Trading Post or the Ole Indian Trading Post and Museum.

The ghost lore is not too far from the truth. Here is the real story. Edgar Watson lived on an old sugar cane plantation in the area. He was regarded as an unsavory character with a bad reputation. People often whispered that he had killed the well-known outlaw Belle Starr. The rumors did not stop there, as Peter Matthiessen wrote in his series of novels on Watson, that people believed he was responsible for at lest one killing in Key West. Watson himself often told tales of killing 57 people. What was the beginning of the end for Watson was the belief that he regularly chopped up his help and fed them to the sharks. On October 24th, Watson made a trip into town to grab some supplies from Smallwood's Store. When he

pulled his boat up to the docks, he was confronted by a group of men from town. After a few words were exchanged, Watson was gunned down and killed.

Visitors to the quiet rural museum often report being overcome with a sense of uneasiness while on the grounds. Many times the witnesses report that an overwhelming feeling of sorrow or dread washes up on them for no apparent reason.

Several staff members and volunteers told us that, while they had heard the ghostly lore of the area, they had yet to have a personal experience inside the museum. However, they quickly stated that it would not surprise them if spirits were roaming the land due to its sordid background.

It appears that most of the activity and creepy feelings take place outside of the museum on the land where Watson was actually killed. It is unclear as to whether the spirit(s) roaming the grounds is that of Edgar Watson or any of his numerous victims, even though they were not killed at this location.

Edgar Watson is buried in Fort Myers Cemetery in Fort Myers.

The Biltmore Hotel & Resort

Location: Coral Gables, Miami-Dade County, Florida
Address: 1200 Anastasia Avenue, Coral Gables, FL 33134-6339
Phone: (305) 445-8066 Ext. 4306
Toll-Free: 1-800-915-1926
Fax: (305) 913-3158
Email: reservations@biltmorehotel.com
Website: www.biltmorehotel.com

Ghost Lore

We want you to take a minute and picture in your mind a hotel that is overrun with illegal activity. Be sure to picture a hotel filled with seedy men gambling all night into the early hours of the day; visualize beautiful ladies of the night engaging their clients in dark rooms; and keep in mind the place is flowing with booze and drugs. I am sure that when doing this exercise many of you did not picture the Biltmore Hotel. That's because the Biltmore Hotel prides itself on being one of the finest hotels in the country. Perhaps it is true that you can never forget your past, but for the Biltmore Hotel it may be that the past never forgets you.

- Years ago a famous gangster was murdered in the hotel and his spirit continues to haunt the hotel seeking those responsible for his death.

- Phantom music can be heard throughout the hotel.

History

1925 – George Merrick and hotel magnate John McEntee Bowman discussed building a great hotel to accommodate high end visitors of the area. Construction on the Biltmore Hotel began.

1926 – The Biltmore was completed at a cost of over 10 million dollars.

1929 – Famous gangster Fatty Walsh was gunned down while playing cards at the hotel.

1930s – During the economic downturn the hotel stayed open by using the pool for shows of synchronized swimming, diving exhibitions, women in swimsuits, and even alligator wrestling.

1940s – During World War II the government converted the hotel into a military hospital.

1973 – The city of Coral Gables was given ownership of the hotel through the Historic Monuments Act and Legacy of Parks program.

1970s - 1980s – The hotel sat abandoned and gained a greater reputation for being a place where strange things took place.

1983 – The city decided to bring the hotel back to its original splendor. A 55 million dollar renovation took place.

1987 – The hotel was officially re-opened.

1992 – The hotel received new operators, headed by the Seaway Hotels Corporation, that signed a long-term management lease with the city of Coral Gables. Work began to renovate the property and make major repairs.

Currently – The Biltmore Hotel is open to the public.

Source: The Biltmore Hotel

Investigation

Adding to the mysterious legends of the Biltmore is the fact that in 1925 construction on the hotel began on Friday the 13th.

The hotel used to give haunted tours of the building every Thursday night. However, these tours are no longer available, and you should not expect the new staff to talk about the haunting at all. We talked with several staff members who officially told us that the

haunted stories were just made up by young children and they were adamant that the hotel was not haunted. When we asked about the numerous reports from guests and visitors, along with the years of haunted tours, they had no comment.

When the hotel was used as a hospital, many veterans and patients died while staying there. Many of their bodies were storied in the hospital's morgue. Many of the spirits that haunt the hotel today are believed to be the spirits of those who met their fate in the building.

Greg Jenkins, in his book *Florida's Ghostly Legends and Haunted Folklore,* wrote that the most frequently seen ghost at the Biltmore is that of the notorious gangster Thomas "Fatty" Walsh. Fatty operated a very profitable casino and speakeasy on the 13th floor of the hotel.

On March 7th, 1929, Fatty Walsh was murdered in his casino on the 13th floor of the hotel while he was playing cards. Numerous newspapers of the day, including *The Galveston Daily News,*

March 8, 1929, reported the murder had been a retaliation killing from the Rothstein murder in which Fatty was a suspect.

In his day, Fatty was seen with many beautiful women and it is told that Fatty was quite the ladies man. Staff told us that many guests, especially women, will get in the elevator and press the button for their floor. But instead of going to their floor, the elevator takes them to the 13th floor. It is believed that the elevator error is the doing of Fatty's ghost that continues to try to get women up to his room.

Back when the hotel was sitting empty, locals often reported seeing unexplained lights moving through the windows of the hotel. Those who lived nearby reported hearing strange sounds coming from the halls of the mighty hotel.

In their book, *American Hauntings,* Mary Beth Sammons and Robert Edwards give an account from a contractor named Dwight Sidway. Dwight was involved in the renovation of the Biltmore in the 1990s and stated that, "The Biltmore was the most haunted site we ever worked on, bar none."

Guests often report turning off their lights when they set off for bed, only to have someone, or something, turn the switch back on.

On many occasions guests have been walking through the country club building when they hear the phantom sounds of the piano being played. When they look at the piano they often see the ghost of a man who appears to be dressed in clothes from 1920s disappear.

Colony Hotel & Cabana Club

Location: Delray Beach, Palm Beach County, Florida
Address: 525 East Atlantic Avenue, Delray Beach, FL 33483-5323
Phone: (561) 276-4123
Toll-Free: 1-800-552-2363
Fax: (561) 276-0123
Website: www.thecolonyhotel.com/florida

Directions: Take Atlantic Ave. to the east toward the beach and the hotel will be on your left.

Ghost Lore

As more and more hotels get gobbled up by huge worldwide resort chains, those that remain often tend to showcase their unique history. So often these places were constructed and operated by owners who had a true passion for the hotel business. One such case is the beautiful Colony Hotel that has the honor of being family operated for over 75 years. In fact, the family's first hotel operator loves the place so much that he refuses to give up his ownership, even from the grave.

- The ghost of the original owner continues to make his rounds at the hotel making sure that all of the guests are well taken care of.

- Chairs and other hotel furniture will often move on their own as though pushed by some unseen force.

History

1925 – Albert T. Repp hired Martin Luther Hampton to design his new hotel. Hampton was a business associate of Addison Minzer (Minzer also helped design the Hollywood Beach Hotel).

1926 – The Altrep Hotel opened after months of stalling due to an embargo on building material caused by the Florida land boom.

1929 – Mr. Repp lost ownership of his hotel. Due to the depression many hotels were lost to the bank and the Altrep Hotel was one of them.

1935 – The hotel was purchased by Charlie Bowden.

1999 – The hotel decided to stay open year-round. Up until this time the hotel would close for four months during the off-season.

2003 – As part of a hotel-wide renovation, the main fireplace was shipped from Maine.

Currently – The hotel is still operated by Charlie's family.

Investigation

The Colony Hotel is the only hotel in Delray Beach to have survived the depression era. All of the others were torn down years ago.

We spoke with the owner of the hotel who is the granddaughter of Charlie. She stated that most of the ghostly activity that takes place at the hotel is believed to be caused by the ghost of her grandfather.

When the hotel was undergoing recent renovations, they bought new luxury beds for all the rooms. One of the delivery guys was busy unloading the beds when he saw an elderly looking man walk by him. What startled the mover the most was the fact that after the strange man passed him, the man appeared to walk right through a wall and disappear.

One evening a maintenance man was working when he thought he saw several hotel guests dancing in the old hall. The man thought that he must have forgotten about a dance in the hotel that night. Curious, he set off to investigate, yet much to his dismay he found the hall empty.

Another common occurrence that takes place at the hotel is the mysterious low hum of big band music that is heard throughout the hotel. Guests often tell of hearing the sounds of music from the 1920s or 30s being played, but they can never find the source of the music. It should be noted that years ago the hotel was well-known for hosting many elegant dances that featured a live big band.

Florida author Greg Jenkins writes in his book, *Florida's Ghostly Legends and Haunted Folklore,* of a couple who were out walking when they passed by the hotel. As the couple walked by they swore they had seen shadows and lights moving inside the closed building. Of course the only rational explanation was that kids had somehow broken into the hotel. The couple hurried to a pay phone and dialed the police. Police officers quickly arrived at the scene and made a perimeter sweep of the hotel checking for signs of a forced entry. When they came up with nothing, one of the officers ventured inside to find the cause of the excitement. Much to the officer's surprise, the hotel was completely empty, all doors and windows were locked shut, and the alarm system was working properly. As the officer was about to leave, the elevator bell rang. The officer waited, thinking that someone would walk out, yet when the elevator doors opened, they unveiled an empty elevator.

We spoke with the Delray Beach Police Department that informed us that their records showed no call reporting trespassing at the hotel. The told us that the police may have investigated complaints of trespassing at the hotel prior to 1999 (the year when the hotel began staying open all year) but if there were no arrests, these files would not have been kept. The police department is not required to store such case files for life, and often disposes of them after a few years.

Mysterious Cries of Haunted Flight 401

Location: Everglades, Miami-Dade County, Florida

Directions: The location of the crash is approximately 8 miles north of the Tamiami Trail. Pay attention for the moans as you travel along Highway 41 (Tamiami Trail Scenic Highway). You can also stop in at any of the airboat tours and inquire about the crash.

Ghost Lore

Filled with alligators, panthers, wild pigs, and maybe even the Florida Skunk Ape, the Everglades can be a very scary place to visit. But when you add the eerie ghostly cries coming from the dead, the Everglades becomes a "can't miss" destination.

- The area is plagued by the sounds of moaning, and cries for help echo throughout the swampy land.

- The spirits of those who died in a plane crash still haunt the secluded swamps.

History

1972 – On December 29th, Eastern Air Lines Flight 401 crashed in the Florida Everglades killing over 100 people.

Investigation

Trouble on Flight 401 began when the crew noticed a malfunction with the landing gear. The crew was so preoccupied with the landing gear that they failed to monitor the plane's other essential instruments, causing the plane to crash into the Everglades. When all was said and done, 101 people had died.

Immediately after the crash, cleanup and rescue crews were dispatched to the area to look for survivors. The rescue efforts continued for several days, but with each passing day the prospect of finding any additional survivors in the alligator-infested waters were slim. Yet, one evening, searchers heard the moans and cries of someone trapped in the swamp; however, regardless of how long they searched, no one was ever found.

In *Florida Ghostly Legends and Haunted Folklore,* researcher Greg Jenkins tells the story of a man who was part of the rescue team who found exactly what he was looking for—or so he thought. During one evening of wreckage cleanup, the man peered into the dark murky water only to see the bloated white face of one of the crash victims. He hollered for help, telling everyone that he had found one of the bodies. Yet when the rest of the crew got to him, there was absolutely nothing floating in the water.

Tour boat operators often bring unsuspecting tourists to the area of the crash site. Much to their surprise, many of the visitors report hearing the faint moaning of the victims forever trapped in the swamp.

Many of the main parts from the crashed Everglades plane were "recycled" into other planes with disastrous results as reported in John Fuller's book, *The Ghost of Flight 401.*

Hollywood Beach Resort

Location: Hollywood, Broward County, Florida
Address: 101 North Ocean Drive, Hollywood, FL 33019-1728
Phone: (954) 922-4396 or (954) 921-0990
Fax: (954) 920-9480

Directions: The hotel is located right on Hollywood's Oceanfront Boardwalk. From downtown, head toward the beach, turn left on North Ocean Drive and the hotel will be on your right.

Ghost Lore

The Hollywood Beach Hotel is a significant part of the town's history. Having survived Al Capone, the Depression, hurricanes, WWII, and corporate buyouts, the hotel proudly sits as a signature landmark on the boardwalk. With such a grand history, filled with legends and lore, you would expect the staff to embrace the uniqueness of the hotel and share its stories. However, while residents share many stories of the hotel's ghostly legends, the staff remains tightlipped about it, making you wonder just exactly what they are hiding. To find out, book yourself a room and start your own investigation.

- The phantom spirits of two men who were murdered on the seventh floor eternally search the resort looking for their killer.
- The hotel was a favorite hot spot for Al Capone and his colleagues to visit while letting the "heat" die down on them in Chicago.

History

1926 – The hotel was constructed in the popular Mediterranean Revival style by Addison Mizner and George Merrick. (Merrick also constructed the Biltmore Hotel.) The hotel cost over three million dollars to complete.

1940s – During WWII, the hotel was converted into the United States Naval Indoctrination and Training School.

1945 – With the end of the war the hotel decided to change its management team. With this change came numerous renovations to the style of the hotel, including the construction of the largest swimming pool in the U.S.

1987 – The hotel underwent another large renovation project. While the structure got a new face, the hotel got a new name. The name was officially changed to the Hollywood Beach Resort.

2002 – The hotel was purchased by the Wyndham Worldwide Company and became part of the Ramada chain of hotels.

Investigation

If every legend about Al Capone was true he would have spent the night in every single hotel room in Florida. However, Capone did have a home in the area, so it is plausible that he may have visited the hotel for dinner or drinks, but it is unlikely he would have stayed the night, as his own home would have provided him much more security.

It appears that the ghostly legends that surround the hotel have been known for many years. We spoke with several senior members of the community who recalled hearing of the unusual happenings at the hotel since they were kids.

We were unable to find any evidence showing that murders took place inside the hotel, or on the seventh floor. The closest we came to finding a horrendous crime was digging up a newspaper story from 1930 in which a large amount of jewelry was stolen from a wealthy woman's room.

Yet the seventh floor does have a ghostly reputation. An employee informed us that while she has worked at the hotel, several of her fellow workers have had weird experiences on the seventh floor. A friend of hers was cleaning rooms on the seventh floor when she heard footsteps of someone coming up behind her. She thought it was just a guest walking down the hall to the elevator. However, as the footsteps got right behind her, they stopped, but when she turned around no one was there. Other workers talk about having their cleaning carts mysteriously moved and having doors close on their own. Strange noises and phantom apparitions have been spotted on this floor as well.

The Hollywood Historical Society told us that they had no reports in their files of a murder taking place in the hotel. The society also believed that Capone had never stayed at the hotel.

Many investigators have visited the hotel searching for spirits. Often times the investigators have picked up numerous orbs on their film.

Most employees of the hotel refuse to talk about the paranormal legends. We did, however, confirm that a long term employee was witness to several paranormal events, yet he declined to expand on his experience. If you decide to visit the hotel, you may have a hard time gathering information from the staff.

Leach Mansion

Location: Jensen Beach, Martin County, Florida
Address: 1701 Northeast Indian River Drive,
Jensen Beach, FL 34957

Directions: From Jensen Beach take Indian River Rd. to the
south. Turn left at the entrance for the Indian Riverside Park
and go to the north end (left) of the parking lot. If you look to
your left you will see the mansion.

Ghost Lore

Every town has a building or home that people refer to as "the old
haunted house." Most of the time the home is just a run down old
building that has fallen on hard times. But sometimes the building
is truly haunted. The Leach Mansion is one such place that certainly lives up to its ghostly reputation.

- Mysterious cold chills are felt throughout the basement of the building.

- Visitors to the run-down building report hearing unexplained noises while on the property.

- Disembodied lights are often spotted roaming the land around the house.

History

The land that the home sits on is an area called Tuckahoe. It is an ancient Native American gathering place and it is has been considered sacred for many years.

1936 – The mansion was constructed for Willaford Leach and his wife Anne Bates Leach. Mrs. Leach was a Coca-Cola heiress as she was the niece of the original CEO of Coca-Cola, Robert Woodruff. The original name of the home was Tuckahoe.

1940s – The local Red Cross used the pool for swimming lessons, and the home was used to entertain service men and their wives during the war.

1949 – Shortly after a major hurricane Mr. and Mrs. Leach sold the home to the Catholic Church. The site was then used as St. Josephs College.

1972 – The home was purchased by the Florida Institute of Technology (FIT) for nearly four million dollars.

1986 – The FIT school closed down for good. The site sat empty for many years.

1997 – The property was purchased by Martin County.

2002 – The building was placed on the National Register of Historic Places.

2007 – A major benefit was held to raise the estimated 2.5 million dollars needed for the project.

2009 – The planned renovations of the building are set to begin that will turn the building into a multi-use community building.

Currently – Renovations are slowly being completed to the mansion.

Investigation

The building and surrounding area is often referred to as Tuckahoe, FIT mansion, or Mount Elizabeth.

We spoke with numerous residents of town who all knew of the house as the "haunted house." We were able to track stories of the place being haunted back to the 1980s, which coincidentally was the time when the home first sat empty and began to deteriorate.

Many visitors report hearing strange noises coming from the home. These noises range from phantom cries of babies to a strange moaning of some unknown spirit.

We spoke with a young lady who told us that one evening she got together with a group of her friends and decided to venture out to the home to see if all of the legends about the place were true. As they approached the building they noticed what appeared to be lights passing by the windows of the home. The group thought that the lights were nothing more than the flashlights of other legend trippers and thought nothing more of it. It was not until they were inside the building that they discovered that no one else was there.

The basement of the Leach home was often used to entertain visiting guests. The college students continued the tradition of using the basement for parties and social gatherings. Today the basement is the place where a lot of people experience strange activity, as most visitors are overcome with an unexplained cold chill while exploring the basement.

Jupiter Inlet Lighthouse & Museum

Location: Jupiter, Palm Beach County, Florida
Address: Lighthouse Park, 500 Captain Armour's Way, Jupiter, FL 33469-3508
Phone: (561) 747-8380
Website: www.jupiterlighthouse.org

Directions: From US Highway 1 turn east on 707. Take the first right and the lighthouse museum and tour will be straight ahead.

Ghost Lore

We have all seen the scary movie where a family is plagued by unusual paranormal happenings only to find out that their home was built on sacred Native American ground. Well, you don't need to go to Hollywood to find haunted sacred ground, but you do need to visit the Jupiter Lighthouse. No one is sure who or what haunts the lighthouse, but with a history of bloody wars, hurricanes, unmarked graves, and Confederate sympathizers, you may just have to find out for yourself.

- Restless spirits of those killed during one of the many conflicts on the land can be seen roaming the land around the lighthouse.

- The spirits of those buried in unmarked graves refuse to rest peacefully.

History

1838 – After the Battle of Loxahatchee, the Fort Jupiter Reservation was created.

1853 – Congress appropriated $35,000 for the construction of the 105-step, 156-foot-tall lighthouse and construction began.

1855-1858 – Due to numerous attacks from Seminole warriors, construction had to be halted.

1860 – The lighthouse was first lit.

1861 – The light was extinguished when three Confederate sympathizers removed essential parts of the lens, making the lighthouse unusable during the Civil War.

1905 – A radio station was placed at the site by the U.S. Navy.

1939 – The US Coast Guard took control of all U.S. lighthouses.

1959 – The old keeper's house was torn down.

1973 – The Jupiter Inlet Lighthouse was added to the National Register of Historic Places.

1999 – The Loxahatchee River Historical Society began an eight-month restoration campaign that returned the tower to its natural color at a cost of over $850,000.

Currently – The lighthouse is open to the public for tours.

Investigation

The history of the land is filled with bloodshed. For years white settlers and the U.S. Army fought with several Native American tribes. Causalities were recorded on both sides, yet the complete number of those who died remains forever unknown.

Several odd things have taken place to unsuspecting visitors touring the lighthouse. Several people taking the tour have reported
that while they were walking up the lighthouse stairs they felt the
hand of someone touch their shoulder. Yet when they looked to see
who tapped them on their shoulder, no one was around them.

Before you reach the lighthouse, off to the right there sits an old
family burial cemetery. The sign on the plot reads:

Our Babies
We are the stillborn children of
Katherine Armour Wells and Joseph Wells,
Assistant Lighthouse Keeper under Capt. Armour in the 1890s.

Several of the tour guides often tell curious children that a couple
of the bodies in the graveyard remain unknown and unnamed, and
that their restless spirits often pay a visit to the lighthouse during
the night.

Over the years, the lighthouse has been home to mysterious noises
and odd lights. Witnesses report seeing a light move up and down
the stairs of the old lighthouse. Many believe the light is from the
ghostly lantern of the former lighthouse caretaker who continues to
care for the lighthouse. No one is sure as to who or what is haunting the land.

The Dare. If you take the guided tour of the lighthouse, you
will be touched by unseen hands.

Lake Worth Playhouse

Location: Lake Worth, Palm Beach County, Florida
Address: 713 Lake Avenue, Lake Worth, FL 33460-3812
Phone: (561) 586-6410
Email: boxoffice@lakeworthplayhouse.org
Website: www.lakeworthplayhouse.org

Directions: The playhouse is located in downtown Lake Worth on Lake Avenue.

Ghost Lore

Two brothers from Illinois traveled to Florida with the dream of opening their own theatre. Once the brothers made to it Lake Worth, their dream soon became a reality. Yet, plagued with bloated costs and the onset of the depression, their dream business soon transformed into a swirling nightmare of continuous bills and struggle. Due to the constant stress of the theatre, one brother began to slide into a terrible state of depression. Unfortunately, he was unable to recover from this, and took his own life at the end of a rope while inside the theatre. The other brother was understandably devastated by the suicide, and exactly one year later he succumbed to a heart attack and joined his brother in death. The spirits of the two brothers still haunt the theatre they loved so dearly.

- Visitors and workers often get a sense that they are not alone while in the theatre and feel as though someone, or something, is watching their every move.

- The mysterious scent of women's perfume permeates throughout the theatre.

History

1924 – Lucian and Clarence Oakley, two brothers from Illinois, began construction on the Oakley Theatre. Right from the beginning their theatre seemed doomed, as construction and labor cost quickly skyrocketed. The brothers had originally planned to spend $46,000 on the business.

1924 – The Oakley Theatre celebrated its grand opening. Newspapers of the day reported that the total cost of the theatre was nearly $150,000. The first show to be featured at the theatre was "Welcome Stranger."

1928 – The town was torn apart by a major hurricane. The theatre suffered tremendous damage and was all but destroyed.

1929 – Destined to make a go of the business, the brothers regrouped and decided to repair the theatre. Several months later the theatre was further upgraded when new state-of-the-art sound and projection equipment were installed.

1930s – Within the span of one year both brothers were dead. Lucian committed suicide and Clarence died exactly one year later.

1940 to 1950s – Numerous times throughout this period the theatre changed ownership. With each new owner came a new name. Many of the owners did not maintain the upkeep and the theatre started to suffer. Finally, the dilapidated theatre was shut down.

1953 – The Lake Worth Playhouse Group was incorporated. The main purpose of the group was to support and preserve the theatre.

1975 – The Lake Worth Playhouse purchased the building for $60,000. The group had been looking for a permanent location for the theatre group.

Currently – The Lake Worth Playhouse continues to entertain the community.

Source: Lake Worth Playhouse

Investigation

The ghost lore on this case is partially true, as Lucian Oakley did commit suicide. However, he did not hang himself in the theatre as

is often erroneously reported. In 1931, Lucian shot himself at his home in Lake Worth.

The theatre has had a long history of being a place where strange things happen. Reports of objects moving on their own, odd smells, and feelings of being watched have been talked about for years.

While spending time in the theatre, many people have caught a glimpse of the ghost of a man who appears to be dressed as though he is from the 1920s or '30s. Witnesses believe the man is the ghost one of the Oakley brothers.

One such person who caught a glimpse of "Oakley" was a former employee who told us that she was up in the control room getting the equipment ready for a show when she was suddenly overcome with the eerie feeling that someone was behind her. As she nervously turned around, the woman saw the ghost of a man disappear into thin air.

Odd smells are one of the more baffling events to take place in the theatre. It is very common for visitors and staff to catch a whiff of a woman's perfume moving around the theatre. Upon investigation no cause for the out of place smell can be found.

Jack Powell writes in his book, *Haunting Sunshine,* that the theatre's dressing rooms are home to many unexplainable events. Powell writes that a woman was sitting in the dressing room getting ready for a show and was putting the finishing touches on her costume, when from behind her she heard a male voice call out her name. Thinking she was alone in the room, the puzzled woman quickly spun around to find that the room was completely empty.

Miami River Inn

Location: Miami, Miami-Dade County, Florida
Address: 118 Southwest South River Drive,
Miami, FL 33130-1419
Phone: (305) 325-0045
Fax: (305) 325-9227
Toll-Free: 1-800-HOTEL89 or 1-800-468-3589
Email: info@miamiriverinn.com
Website: www.miamiriverinn.com

Directions: The inn is on the corner of S.W. 2nd Street &
S.W. 4th Avenue. From the north, take exit #1B (S.W. 7th
Street). Turn right at S.W. 7th Street. Turn right at S.W. 5th
Avenue. Make another right at S.W. 2nd Street and the inn will
be on your left.

Ghost Lore

Throughout this guide you will find many places that are a hotbed of paranormal occurrences. For many of them it is easy to figure out why, as they often have a tragic past involving murder, suicide, death, sadness and sorrow. But what about places where the history seems to be both normal and mundane? Can these "normal" places be haunted, too? The answer is . . . . Well, spend a night at the historic Miami River Inn and then decide for yourself.

- The unknown spirit of a woman walks the grounds of this historic inn.

- Bizarre noises can be heard from many of the guestrooms.

History

1906 to 1913 – The nine buildings were constructed.

For a time, several of the buildings were private homes while others were used as guesthouses.

1987 – Led by local preservationist Sallye Jude, the hotel was renovated and brought back to the magnificent condition of its past.

1987 – The buildings were placed on the National Register of Historic Places as part of the South River Drive Historic District.

Little else is known about the history of the inn.

Investigation

We spoke with a house keeper who had an odd experience while cleaning one of the guest rooms. As per her usual routine, she had left the front door of the room open along with the bedroom and bathroom doors. As she was busy cleaning, out of nowhere, all three doors suddenly slammed shut at the exact same time. The woman was exteremely puzzled as she noticed that there was absolutely no breeze outside.

Several guests have reported seeing the apparition of a young woman decked out in a long flowing white dress walking around the property. The identity of this strange woman remains a mystery.

We spoke with the management of the inn who informed us that they are not aware of any tragic events or deaths that have taken place at the inn.

Throughout the years, workers and guests at the inn would often hear the sound of footsteps coming from empty upstairs rooms.

It is a common experience for visitors and staff to hear the sound of heavy furniture slowly being moved across the floor. As the banging and dragging continues, visitors inform the staff of the odd noise. The staff set off to check out the noise, only to discover that the "noisy" room is empty.

Villa Paula Mansion

Location: Miami, Miami-Dade County, Florida
Address: 5811 North Miami Avenue, Miami, FL 33127-1625

Directions: From Hwy 95, exit east on Dr. Martin Luther King Jr. Blvd. (NW 62nd St.). Turn right on N. Miami Ave. and the Villa Paula will be on your right.

Note: *Private Property. Please view from road.*

Ghost Lore

It is not surprising that a home in "Little Haiti" would have bizarre legends surrounding it, as Haiti is home to many bizarre voodoo stories, but the building featured in this story is Cuban, not Haitian. There are so many strange events that have happened in the home that no one is sure of the cause. However, others remain convinced that they know what is causing the activity at the home, and her name is Paula.

- The home is haunted by the angry spirit of a woman who died of mysterious causes while living in the home.

- The property has a hatred for animals and any cat that finds its way on the land will meet death through a bizarre accident.

History

1916 – The first Cuban consulate was constructed in Miami due to the request of several of Miami's lumber barons who had been doing business with Cuba for several years. The building is no longer standing.

1926 – The Villa Paula was designed by architect C. Freira. It was constructed by the Cuban government to serve as the Cuban consulate. Adding to the uniqueness of this building is the fact that it was constructed entirely with materials brought from Cuba. The Villa was named Paula, the wife of Domingo Milord, who was the chancellor of the Cuban consulate.

1930 – Milord sold the building to Helen Reardon. Helen and her two daughters lived in the building.

1960s – The home was empty and was a favorite hangout for partying kids and drifters that needed a place to crash for the night.

1974 – Cliff Ensoh and S. L. Sharlow purchased the home.

1976 – Numerous newspapers around the country carried the story of the Villa Paula being put up for sale, and that a ghost came with it.

1985 – The building was auctioned off.

There are currently rumors circulating that the building is going to be turned into a Cuban museum.

Source: Miami Heritage Conservation Board

Investigation

It is widely believed that the home is haunted by Paula Milord. Local legend states that Paula died under mysterious conditions while suffering terribly in her room. How much of the local legend is true? First, Paula did not die in the house. A *Key West Citizen* newspaper article from August 26th, 1932 stated that on August 10th Paula had taken ill and was rushed to the Jackson Memorial Hospital in Miami. However, nothing the doctors did for her seemed to help, as her condition continued to deteriorate. Finally, on August 25th, Paula could not hang on any longer, and she was pronounced dead in her hospital room.

In 1976, dozens of newspapers around the U.S. ran stories stating that the home was for sale. What made the story unique was that

the owner at that time, Cliff Ensoh, stated that a ghost came with the sale of the place.

The March 31st edition of the *Florida Playground Daily News* reported that the ghost of the house was considered a troublemaker until Mr. Ensoh stood in the middle of his bedroom and said, "Paula, I don't mind your living here, but you have to be peaceable."

Throughout the house, witnesses would see shadows appear on the wall as though they were living objects. Without fail the shadows always disappeared as soon as they were noticed.

A guest spending the night at the Villa woke up one evening, rubbed his eyes, and was amazed to see the ghost of a woman walking inside the house. The ghost was said to be that of a tall woman with olive skin and beautiful long black hair that had been pulled tight behind her head. The woman appeared wearing a black gown that was decorated with ruffles around the neck and sleeves. Others have heard the sound of women's high heels walking through the house, yet no cause can ever be found.

One evening, the owner heard the sound of someone scuffling through the kitchen. Curious as to what could have made the noise, he rushed to the kitchen, only to find that while the cutlery was scattered all over the floor, the room was mysteriously empty.

Michael Norman and Beth Scott, in their book, *Historic Haunted America,* write that on several occasions the cats of the home had been strangled by a heavy iron gate that inexplicably closed shut on them.

The Dare. To simply walk past the house on the sidewalk. Neighborhood children are terrified to walk past the home and many refuse to do so.

Glenn H. Curtiss Mansion

Location: Miami Springs, Miami-Dade County, Florida
Address: Glenn H. Curtiss Mansion, 500 Deer Run,
Miami Springs, FL 33166-5852

Directions: The mansion is located next to the Miami Springs
Golf and Country Club. From 36th St., take the Curtiss
Parkway (NW 57th Ave). Follow to Deer Run and turn right.
At the corner of Deer Run and La Baron Dr. the mansion will
be on your right. Follow the narrow road to the mansion.

Ghost Lore

Glen Curtiss was a world famous aviation pioneer. What many
people did not know about him is that he also loved kids. He had
such a warm heart for needy children that he transformed half of his
mansion into a functioning daycare. The story deepens when his
wife found out that she was pregnant and decided to have a secret
abortion. When Curtiss found out about the abortion he was dev-

astated, but his hurt soon turned to anger and he lashed out at his wife. In retaliation for his action, his wife took a match to the mansion and burned it down while Curtiss was inside.

- Late at night sounds of horrific screams echo throughout the neighborhood.

- Unexplained balls of light have been seen floating around the home.

History

1925 – Curtiss, a well-known land developer and aviator in Florida, wanted to construct a home in Miami Springs. Curtiss hired the well-known architect Martin Luther Hampton to design his home.

1930 – Curtiss passed away in New York. His wife Lena Curtiss continued to live in their home. Eventually she was remarried to a man named H. Sayre Wheeler, who happened to be an old business partner of her deceased husband. The couple continued to live in the home until the 1940s.

1953 – The home was sold and work soon began that would transform the home into the Miami Springs Villa.

1970s – The Miami Springs Villa was sold to Forte Hotels Inc.

1987 – The building was designated as a Miami Springs Historic Site.

1994 – Vandals started a fire that destroyed much of the inside of the mansion.

1994 to 1998 – The mansion sat empty, which attracted vandals and trespassers.

1998 – The dilapidated mansion was donated to the city of Miami Springs.

2001 – The home was placed on the National Register of Historic Places.

Currently – The city is the process of raising money to renovate the mansion, with the intent of using it as a cultural center and museum.

Investigation

Glen Curtiss was not burned to death by his vengeful wife. In 1930, Curtiss died in Buffalo, New York due to complications after undergoing appendicitis surgery.

We were unable to find any evidence to suggest that Mrs. Curtiss had an abortion. However, it is unlikely that she would have had an abortion, as the couple did have two children together. If Mrs. Curtiss did have an illegal abortion (abortion became legal in 1973), it was a secret that was never known by many of her friends and staff.

We spoke with a historian at the Miami Springs Historical Museum who told us that her father was employed at the mansion for over ten years. She also debunked the story of the original fire and subsequent abortion.

Perhaps the story of a 1920's mansion fire was developed after vandals burned the mansion in 1994. Since 1994, two other illegal fires have plagued the mansion, destroying nearly all of the inner structure.

We spoke to the Miami Springs Police Department, where police records confirm that arson reports were filled in 1997 and 1999. The officers also told us that over the years the number of calls regarding people trespassing in the mansion has diminished.

Residents often will be outside at night in their yards when they are startled by the sounds of someone playing tennis at the mansion. Knowing that the mansion should be closed down, they go to investigate, and they find that the property is completely empty.

Tales of dark, sinister screams coming from mansion have been circulating for over 50 years.

For years the once grand mansion sat empty. As it continued to deteriorate, it gained a wider reputation as being haunted. Many visitors reported that strange balls of lights could be seen hovering inside the mansion. Observers could watch, as these unknown lights moved passed windows and open doors.

During an investigation at the mansion, the Florida Ghost Team reported that they had captured unexplained voices on their equipment.

Flagler Museum

Location: Palm Beach, Palm Beach County, Florida
Physical Address: Henry Morrison Flagler Museum,
One Whitehall Way, Palm Beach, FL 33480-4065
Mailing Address: P.O. Box 969, Palm Beach, FL 33480-0969
Phone: (561) 655 2833
Fax: (561) 655 2826
Email: mail@flaglermuseum.us
Website: www.flaglermuseum.us

Directions: From Highway 1 heading north, turn right on Loftin St. (Flagler Memorial Bridge). Turn right on Cocoanut Row. Turn right on Whitehall Way and you will see the museum.

Ghost Lore

Have you ever struggled to find the perfect birthday, Christmas, or wedding present for someone? If you were one of the wealthiest men in America, would it make the process any easier? Well, Henry Flagler was in such a position. He decided to give his new wife a beautiful 55-room mansion for a wedding present. Flagler had the mansion constructed to be one of the finest buildings in the entire world and could not have known that one day the mansion would be responsible for his death. His wife absolutely loved her new home—so much so, that even death could not get her to leave.

- A mysterious spirit peering out of the second floor window often scares those walking the pathway to the home.

- The ghost of a former owner is still seen on the staircase where he met his fate nearly 100 years ago.

History

1901 – The mansion was constructed for Henry Flagler. The mansion served as the wedding gift for his third wife, Mary Lily Kenan Flagler. The same architects that designed his home in St. Augustine (John Carrere and Thomas Hastings) were commissioned for the design of his new home.

1913 – Flagler passed away after an accident in the mansion. After his death, the home remained closed until 1916.

1917 – Mary Lily passed away under mysterious circumstances, and left the home to her niece, Louise Clisby Wise Lewis.

1925 – Ms. Lewis sold the mansion. The new owners quickly added a 10-story, 300-room tower to be used as a luxury hotel.

1959 – After years of wear and tear, the building was in need of major repairs and it was on the verge of being torn down. Flagler's granddaughter, Jean Flagler, got wind of the condition of the home and helped form a non-profit group called The Henry Morrison Flagler Museum.

1960 – The home was once again open to the public, as the museum group held an elegant "Restoration Ball," to raise funds for the renovation of the building.

Currently – The mansion is used as a museum and is open to the public for tours.

Investigation

It is true that in 1913 Flagler suffered a tragic accident when he tumbled down the stairs at his mansion. He never did fully recover from his fall and passed away soon after.

Although Mary Lily Kenan was nearly 40 years younger than Flagler, she followed him into death in 1917. Mary died under mysterious conditions just eight months after marrying Robert Worth Bingham. Her death set off tales of poisoning, murder, and conspiracy theories which continue to this day.

In years past, many of the museum's workers were open to discussing the stories and legends of the mansion. Many of them would even swap tales of their own personal experiences.

We spoke with several of the administrative staff who refused to talk about the haunting, lending ever more mystery to the property.

The second floor is home to many odd sightings. The most common sighting is that of the ghost of Mary standing by the second floor window, keeping an eye out for any newly arriving visitors. Those who have spotted her state that she will disappear right before your eyes.

Much of the paranormal activity is attributed to the spirit of Mary Kenan. On numerous occasions an apparition of a woman has been seeing floating through the home. The woman's fancy flowing gown and large elegant hat makes her appear as though she is from a time period long since passed.

Mary is certainly not alone, as Henry Flagler is also said to be haunting his former home. Visitors touring the mansion often see the ghost of a well-dressed elderly man slowly struggling to walk up and down the staircase where Flagler met his fate. Those who witness this unusual sight are convinced that it is indeed the ghost of Henry Flagler.

The Dare. If you look up at any second-story window you will see the spirit of Mary peering down at you with an evil judgmental stare.

The Devil's Tree

Location: Port Saint Lucie, Saint Lucie County, Florida
Address: Oak Hammock Park, 1982 Southwest Villanova
Road, Port Saint Lucie, FL 34953-1325
Phone: (772) 878-2277

Directions

To the Park: Head west on SW California Blvd. Turn left at
SW Pamona St. Turn right at SW Leisure Lane. Turn left at
SW Ruiz Terrace. SW Ruiz Terrace will turn right and
becomes SW Leafy Rd. Take a left at SW Villanova Rd.
(From California Blvd. there will be signs.)

To the Tree - Scary Way: Take the Oak Trail to the left; there
will be a small pond on your left. The trail will then curve to the
right. At the Y take the trail to the left, and you will pass by a
small bench on each side of you. At the beige bench, curve
left and go straight until the blue post and turn right. The tree
will be on your right. It is full of carvings, paint, etc.

Non-Scary Route: Head toward the Oak Trail. Go to the right along the water canal. Take your first left at the blue post and the tree will be straight ahead on the left.

Ghost Lore

Many years ago, a deranged killer was prowling Port St. Lucie when he came upon two young women walking in the area. The women were soon beaten and sexually assaulted. The man then took the motionless bodies and hung them from a tree to admire his work. Wanting to save his blood-soaked trophies, he quickly buried the bodies of the women under the tree for later use. It is believed that for years the man would often come back to the tree and dig up the bodies for a night of demented fun. Several years later, two men stumbled upon the rotting ropes and noticed the remains of the women.

- No matter what method is used, the tree cannot be cut down.

- The spirits of two young women continue to haunt the tree where they met their eternal fate.

- Mysterious robed figures often perform satanic rituals at the death site.

History

1973 – Barbara Ann Wilcox and Colette Marie Goodenough were reported missing.

1973 – Gerald Schaefer was convicted for the murders of Susan Place and Georgia Jessup. Schaefer had tied them to a tree where he sexually assulted and tortured them.

1977 – The bodies of Barbara Ann Wilcox and Colette Marie Goodenough were discovered in Port St. Lucie.

1995 – Schaefer was found stabbed to death in his prison cell.

233

Investigation

Unfortunately, the ghost lore of this case is pretty much true. In 1973, roommates Barbara Ann Wilcox and Colette Marie Goodenough went missing from their apartment in Iowa. The 19-year-old girls were last seen in Mississippi hitchhiking to Florida. In 1977, the bodies of the two women were found scattered in the area that would become Oak Hammock Park in Port St. Lucie. No cause of death could be found. Although no one was ever charged in their murder, there is little doubt that the girls were just two of the many victims of serial killer Gerard Schaefer. In a search of Schaefer's home, Police retrieved Barbara's driver's license, and Collette's passport and diary. Schaefer was convicted of killing two women and is thought to have killed many, many more.

Because the case was never solved, researchers are not exactly sure what happened to the women in the park. However, based on published reports on what Schaefer did to his other victims, we can surmise that the girls were brought to the area and hung up against a

tree with a rope while Schaefer threatened, tortured, and sexually abused them. According to researcher Michael Newton, Schaefer liked to make his pairs of victims fight over who would be killed first.

We found no evidence to support the story of the two women being buried in the ground so that Schaefer could come back and dig up and ravage their corpses. The bones of the two women were actually found scattered throughout the surrounding bushes. Yet, on the other hand, what really took place out there remains an unsolved mystery and might be a tale of unspeakable horrors best left untold.

It is said that over the years many people have unsuccessfully tried to cut down the tree. Each time an effort was made to get rid of the tree, the equipment would mysteriously fail to function, thus leaving the tree standing.

We have received dozens of similar reports from people who visit the tree and get a bit more than they bargained for. The reports almost always go something like this:

> My friends and I drove out to see the Devil's Tree in Port St. Lucie. Once we got we started to make our way to the tree when we heard the faint cry of a woman. As we got closer to the tree the voice became louder and we figured that it was another group of people who got spooked at seeing the tree. Yet when we got to the tree, we found that there was no one else there.

Numerous sightings of unknown figures dressed in cloaks and hooded robes have been reported at the tree. The local legend states that these people were involved in some type of satanic rituals. In his book, *Weird Florida*, Charlie Carlson includes a story about a group of friends camping out in the park. While the group was camping one evening they spotted several people "wearing hoods and robes" near the tree. Later, the witnesses were told that the people they had seen were warlocks performing a ritual.

We spoke with several young residents of Port St. Lucie who warned us not to go out to the park at night by ourselves. They told us that on numerous occasions they had gone out to the Devil's Tree at night, and each time they approached the tree they were overcome with a sense of dread, and an unexplained cold chill passed over their bodies as they fled the area in terror.

SOUTHWEST FLORIDA

May-Stringer Heritage Museum

Location: Brooksville, Hernando County, Florida
AKA: The Hernando Heritage Museum
Physical Address: 601 Museum Court,
Brooksville, FL 34601-2631
Mailing Address: P.O. Box 12233,
Brooksville, FL 34603-2233
Phone: (352) 799-0129
Fax: (352) 796-6766
Email: raidplace@earthlink.net
Website: www.hernandoheritagemuseum.com

Directions: From Brooksville take E. Fort Dade Ave. to the east. Turn right onto Museum Court, and the house will be on your right.

Ghost Lore

Most haunted places have just a few odd events that happen, yet the

May-Stringer home seems to a have a complete laundry list of bizarre activity taking place including:

- Lights that mysteriously turn on and off on their own.

- A phantom smell of fresh-baked pie that permeates throughout the home.

- The spirit of a young girl who eerily cries out for her mother.

- Toys that move on their own as though played with by some unseen presence.

- The sounds of unknown people walking around in the empty attic.

History

1856 – A basic frame house was constructed by Mr. John May. When completed, the home contained two bedrooms, a parlor, a dining room, and an unattached kitchen.

1866 to 1872 – May's widow Marena re-married a man named Frank Saxon who also occupied the home with her during this period. Sometime during this period the couple had a son that died five weeks after birth.

1869 – The couple gave birth to a daughter named Jessie May Saxon. Marena died while giving birth to Jessie.

1872 – Jessie May Saxon passed away at the age of three.

1880s – Dr. Sheldon Stringer purchased the property and home.

1903 – The house underwent some major renovations and was altered into a Queen Anne style home.

1981 – The home was purchased by Hernando County Historical Museum.

1997 – The home was added to the National Register of Historic Places.

Currently – The building is home to the Hernando Heritage Museum and is open to the public.

Source: Hernando Heritage Museum and the self-guided walking tour of the city of Brookville's historical homes.

Investigation

When visiting the museum people often hear the faint voice of a young girl crying out "mommy, mommy." These eerie cries are thought to come from the spirit of young Jessie May Saxon. Jessie was only three years old when she passed away inside the home, and it is believed that her spirit is eternally searching for her lost mother.

The museum staff often report that before closing up for the day they routinely make a last check of the home to make sure everything is put away in the proper area. In the morning when the workers return they are amazed to discover that many of the toys have been scattered around the floor as though someone or something had been playing with them during the night.

A 2007 article in the *St. Petersburg Times* reported that the home was plagued with mysterious noises. In addition to the ghostly cries, the unaccounted for sounds of toddlers, barking dogs, banging pipes, and phantom footsteps have all been reported.

We spoke with several staff members who told us that on many occasions visitors have strolled up to the porch and were about to enter the house when they were overcome with an uncomfortable feeling that they could not explain and they refused to enter the house.

When asked, several of the staff said they believed that the unknown spirits may be attached to one of the hundreds of antiques that furnish the home.

Madira Bickel Mound State Archeological Site

Location: Ellenton, Manatee County, Florida
Address: 3708 Patten Avenue, Ellenton, FL 34222-2152
Phone: (941) 723-4536

Directions: From St. Petersburg head south on I-275 to
Palmetto. Take a right at the Highway 19 exit. From 19 turn
right on Terra Ceia Rd. This will turn into Bayshore Drive.
Stay on Bayshore for approximately 2 miles, and the park will
be on your right. Follow the stairs up to the mound.

Ghost Lore

In the middle of several new housing developments rests a sacred
1000-year-old Native American burial and worship site. As you
walk back to the mound, you will be overcome with the sense that
"other" people are there with you, safely guiding you through the
ancient grounds.

History

1000 BCE to 500 CE – The large ceremonial mound and burial land was built by local Native Americans of the area.

1900 – C. B. Moore measured the mound and found that it was 99 by 169 feet at the base and its height was over 20 feet.

1914 – Development in the area caused sand from the mound to be removed and used for road fill. Workers of that time reported finding several human bones among the mound.

1930 – Digging into the moundled to the discovery of many pieces of assorted pottery.

1948 – The mound and surrounding 10 acres of property were donated to the state of Florida by Karl and Madira Bickel and Mrs. R.H. Prine.

1951 – A partial excavation of the mound showed that it was comprised of alternating layers of sand and shell.

1970 – The park was added to the National Register of Historical Places.

Source: Florida State Parks and the School District of Manatee County

Investigation

Researchers believe the mound may have been the site of a village called Ucita. The site is considered a sacred site by Native Americans and should be treated as such.

Those who visit the mound often report getting a sense that they are not alone. Feelings that you are being watched and followed by some unseen spirit are common at the site. Even those with no psychic ability report feeling that the place is special and sacred.

It is believed that visitors are feeling the presence of the spirits of those who are buried in the area. These protective spirits are said to roam the area to ensure the safety of the mound.

The Artist House

Location: Key West, Monroe County, Florida
Address: 534 Eaton Street, Key West, FL 33040-6881
Phone: (305) 296-3977
Toll-Free: 1-800-582-7882
Fax: (305) 296-3210
Email: info@artisthousekeywest.com
Website: www.artisthousekeywest.com

Directions: The home is on Eaton Street in Historic Downtown Key West.

Ghost Lore

Bed and breakfasts are often beautiful historic homes that offer their guests an opportunity to relax and enjoy the marvelous antiques and history of these majestic homes. With seven wonderful rooms filled with antique furnishings The Artist House is certainly no exception. What separates The Artist House from a regular run of the mill B&B is the unique history that goes along with it. I am sure you will find the home's history a bit odd, unless of course you do not consider cursed voodoo dolls, phantom apparitions, and protective ghosts as being odd.

- A possessed doll spent years in the home terrorizing the occupants.

- A mysterious woman floats down the spiral staircase.

- The spirit of a former occupant has come back to protect the home from evil spirits.

History

1890 to 1898 – The Artist House was constructed in a Colonial Queen Anne style.

1898 – Mr. and Mrs. Thomas Otto and their three children moved into the new home.

1904 – Robert the Doll was given to artist Robert "Gene" Otto by servant, probably of Bahamian or Hatian descent, when he was a small child.

1930 – Gene, the youngest of the three children, married Annette Parker of Boston.

1930s – Gene and his new wife moved back to his childhood home in Key West.

1974 – Gene passed away while inside the Turret Room. Annette moved back to Massachusetts and the home was sold to Myrtle and William Reuter, and Robert the doll came with it.

1976 – Annette passed away. The home was purchased by Nancy Tazwell.

1994 – Nancy Tazwell donated Robert to the East Martello Museum.

Currently – The home is owned by David Wilson and Sanford Berris.

Investigation

Robert the doll was given to young Gene as a present. While growing up, like most kids, Gene would get into trouble. However, every time something went wrong Gene would blame it on the doll saying, "Robert did it." Throughout his life Gene kept a close bond with Robert and even gave the doll its own room overlooking the street. In his later years Gene was often very abusive to his wife. Gene would often burst into fits of rage and then suddenly snap out of it and say that it was all Robert's fault.

One of the theories is that Robert was given to Gene by a Bohemian or Haitian woman that had put a voodoo spell on the doll.

Robert originally was given a room to himself in the attic. Legend states that Gene told his wife that Robert was angry for being trapped inside the cramped attic and that he demanded that he be given a room with a better view. To satisfy Robert's demands, Gene moved Robert to the Turret Room and placed him next to the window.

Passersby to the house often were stunned when the reported seeing Robert moving throughout the room. Many young children had an odd feeling that Robert was watching their every move as they passed the home.

A plumber was called in to do some repairs in the Turret Room. Soon after arriving the man fled the house in terror. When asked why he left without finishing the job, he stated that he had heard Robert giggling at him.

Former occupants reported hearing the sounds of someone running around in the attic and when they went to investigate they found Robert was on the other side of the room.

Although Robert is no longer housed in The Artist House, many strange events still take place in the historic home and some believe that his spirit remains at the home.

We spoke with the staff that informed us that they are reluctant to venture into the attic for fear of what may happen.

Gene's wife Annette is the spirit most often seen roam through the house. She is usually seen walking down the spiral staircase from the Turret Room. She is always seen wearing what appears to be her wedding dress. It is believed to be protecting the home from Robert.

Guests have also reported seeing the ghost of an older looking gentleman moving inside the house. The ghost is believed to be that of Gene Otto who continues to walk the home where he lived for most of his life.

Captain Tony's Saloon

Location: Key West, Monroe County, Florida
Address: 428 Greene Street, Key West, FL 33040-6567
Phone: (305) 294-1838
Website: www.capttonyssaloon.com

Directions: Located on Greene Street in the historic downtown of Key West.

Ghost Lore

Captain Tony's Saloon is one of those rare places where you immediately feel at ease. This could be why so many famous people have been drawn to the saloon. Ernest Hemingway, Truman Capote, Jimmy Buffett, and Presidents Harry Truman and John Kennedy have all stopped in to enjoy this historic saloon. Yet the most famous of Tony's patrons are not celebrities or politicians. In fact, most people do not even know their names. What people do know is that these people are dead and it is their spirits that continue to enjoy the relaxing atmosphere of Tony's, even from the grave.

- The spirits of those who are buried under the foundation of the bar continue to roam the building seeking eternal rest.

- A woman in a blue blood-spattered dress is seen walking throughout the bar.

- Holy water was placed inside the walls and floor in order to keep the spirits from haunting the area.

History

1800s – The building was used as the town's first morgue.

1890 – A wireless telegraph station occupied the building on Greene Street. Often important news was sent from this office to locations around the world.

1912 – The building was used as a cigar factory. Shortly after this, the building was transformed into a bar and brothel. The "ladies of the night" catered to mostly Navy men.

1916 – On August 10th, Anthony "Tony" Tarracino was born in Elizabeth, New Jersey to a bootlegger father.

1930 – At the end of prohibition, Joe "Josie" Russell purchased the business. Josie also ran a little speakeasy on Duval Street.

1933 – Josie decided to move his speakeasy from Duval St. to his new building. Josie had nearly three times the space of his former building.

1933 – Sloppy Joe's at 428 Green Street was officially opened and quickly became the favorite watering hole of Ernest Hemingway.

1938 – A dispute over a rent increase of $4 caused Josie to move the entire bar across the street. A clause in the contract that allowed the landlord to keep all fixtures forced Josie to move his bar in the

middle of the night. He ended up bringing all the fixtures with him, including the lights.

1940 – The building was re-opened as a bar called the "Duval Club" and was owned by Morgan Bird. Known for throwing gay themed parties, the club was soon put on the Navy "do not visit" list and the lack of business forced it to close shortly after.

1948 – Tony Tarracino became a gambler, but was caught cheating the New Jersey Mafia who beat him and left him for dead in a land-fill. Shortly thereafter, he moved to Key West and became known as "Captain Tony" when he worked as a charter boat captain—a job he held for 35 years.

1958 – Tarracino purchased the former Duval Club building from David Wolkowsky and named the bar "Captain Tony's Saloon."

1970s – Singer and songwriter Jimmy Buffet performed there regularly. Tarracino and Buffet became close friends.

1985 – Tarracino's life was memorialized by Buffett in the song "Last Mango in Paris."

1986 – Captain Tony sold the bar, but it continued to bear his name.

1989 – Tarracino was elected mayor of Key West and served for two terms.

1995 – He had open-heart surgery.

2008 – On November 1st, Captain Tony died of lung and heart ailments in Key West at the age of 92. He was married four times and had thirteen children.

Currently – Captain Tony's Saloon is still open and a frequent stop on the ghost tours of Key West.

Source: www.capttonyssaloon.com

Investigation

Captain Tony's is the oldest licensed saloon in Florida.

The building served as the first morgue in Key West. The coroner at the time, Joseph Edmunds, buried his daughter Elvira on the land. Her gravestone can be viewed in the floor of the pool room. Captain Tony and his workers discovered the remains of Elvira and 15 others while laying the foundation for the bar. Tony left the gravestone visible, partly as a reminder of the history and partly out of respect for the dead so they wouldn't haunt the place.

Construction workers that unearthed the bodies were so terrified by their grisly find that they went about filling empty Coke bottles with holy water and placing them in the walls and floor in order to

appease the disturbed spirits of those who were buried there. In the pool room you can still see various parts of these bottles sticking out of the walls.

Growing through the middle of the bar is a large tree affectionately known as the "Hanging Tree." It was here that years ago thieves, murderers, and pirates met their fate at the end of a rope. The true number of people hanged from this tree is lost to time, yet depending on who you believe, the number ranges from 5 to 75.

The most active spirit in the bar seems to be a woman who was hanged from the tree for murder. Years back the woman was convicted of killing her husband and children. When she was apprehended she was wearing the blood-soaked dress from the killings. When she was finally hanged, the woman's neck did not immedi-

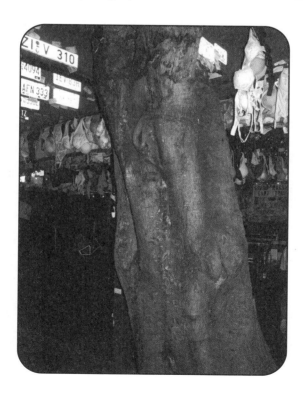

ately break, which left her hanging there to face a slow excruciating death.

Although the spirit of the hanged woman has been spotted throughout the saloon, she is mostly seen inside the women's restroom. Witnesses report that she is wearing the same blood-filled blue dress that she was hanged in.

One bartender told us that she often gets women who stop by the tavern in order to use the restroom. On numerous occasions these unsuspecting women came running from the bathroom to ask the bartender if the place was haunted, because they had just witnessed the spirit of the dead woman in the restroom. In addition to many people seeing the spirit of the woman, others simply feel her presence while they are in the saloon.

Staff told us that people who take photographs of the hanging tree are often surprised to find that they have captured mysterious orbs and mist on their pictures.

The Ghost Of Ernest Hemingway

Location: Key West, Monroe County, Florida
Address: The Ernest Hemingway Home & Museum,
907 Whitehead Street, Key West, FL 33040-7473
Phone: (305) 294-1136
Email: info@hemingwayhome.com
Website: www.hemingwayhome.com

Directions: The home is on the corner of Whitehead St. and
Truman Ave. in historic downtown Key West.

Ghost Lore

Perhaps the most famous Key West personality is that of Ernest
Hemingway, who first visited Key West in 1929. He immediately
feel in love with the uniqueness of the town and the equally uniqueness of its people. After purchasing a home in Key West,
Hemingway spent his days writing and his nights playing. He trav-

eled around town with a group of friends looking for drinks and adventure. Of course, he easily found them both in the town's many corners. After his death many vowed to keep his spirit alive in Key West . . . little did they know that Hemingway intended to do the same!

- The ghost of Hemingway is often seen walking around his home much like he did while he was alive.

- Mysterious noises are heard throughout the museum, causing the staff to wonder if Hemingway continues to write from the grave.

- The museum is home to cats that all have six toes.

History

1851 – The home was constructed by Asa Tift, who was a marine architect.

1899 – The famous writer Ernest Hemingway was born in Oak Park, Illinois.

1927 – He married Pauline Pfeiffer.

1931 – The home was purchased by Hemingway.

1930s – Key West's first pool was constructed. At a cost of $20,000, Hemingway was a bit upset. He apparently took a penny from his pocket and jokingly said, "Here, take the last penny I've got," and threw it in the wet cement. The penny is still there today.

1959 – Hemingway's wife Pauline died. The fully furnished house was rented out.

1961 – Hemingway committed suicide in Ketchum, Idaho at the age of 62.

1961 – After the death of Hemingway, Mrs. Bernice Dickson, a local Key West businesswoman, purchased the home from his estate.

1964 – Mrs. Dickson opened the home as a museum to the public.

1968 – The home was designated a National Historic Landmark.

Currently – The home is open to the public and is still owned by Mrs. Dickson.

Source: The Hemingway Home and Museum

Investigation

The museum has about 60 cats that roam freely over the grounds, and yes a fair share of them (about 50%) are polydactyl, meaning they have six toes instead of five. They are the descendents of Hemingway's original cats.

Staff members told us that they are aware of the ghostly reputation of the place, and numerous guests have had experiences while at the home.

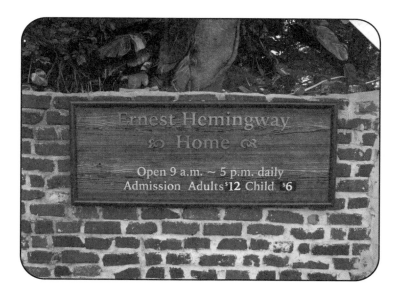

Museum workers told us that numerous guests taking the house tour have reported seeing the ghost of a man that looks exactly like Hemingway sitting in the Boy's Room. When the witnesses turn to get a closer look at the man, they find that he is no longer there.

Often times during the wee hours of the night and the early morning the staff will hear the faint sounds of a phantom typewriter being used. Convinced that no one is in the home, the staff tries to investigate the mysterious noise. After searching the entire home, for the source of the unexplained noise, the staff could not find a cause for the noise.

David Sloan, in his book *Haunted Key West,* told the story of a man down in Key West during Hemingway Days that ventured over the Hemingway's home to get a little closer with the man he admired so much. When he got to the home, he stopped at the gate and stood there for awhile admiring the home and soaking in the feel of what the home and town must have been like when Hemingway lived there. Several minutes later his attention was called to a noise originating from the veranda. Thinking it was the home's caretaker moving about, the man looked up and was surprised to see a man that looked exactly like Hemingway standing there. At first glance the man thought that it was a Hemingway look-a-like getting a private tour so he called out to him, "Hey Ernest," and waved his hand enthusiastically. The man on the veranda apparently saw him waving and waved back. It was then that the man on the street noticed that the Hemingway-looking man was completely transparent and then, right before the man's eyes, Hemingway disappeared into thin air.

Robert the Enchanted Doll

Location: Key West, Monroe County, Florida
Address: The Fort East Martello Museum and Gardens,
3501 South Roosevelt Boulevard, Key West, FL 33040-5209
Phone: (305) 296-3913
Website: www.kwahs.com/martello.htm

Directions: The museum is located right next to the airport.
From Highway 1 coming into Key West, turn left (east) on
Highway 1A. Follow this as it becomes S. Roosevelt Blvd. The
museum will be on your right.

Ghost Lore

Do you remember the *Child's Play* movies? Well, the premise of
the movies was simple—the evil spirit of a killer was transferred
into the body of a harmless doll named Chucky. The evil doll then
started to act with its own agenda. Although many people were
scared by this far-fetched story, you can rest assured that scary

dolls with spirits is something that only take place in Hollywood, right? Well you may want to visit Key West to find out for yourself.

- A voodoo curse continues to keep its hold on a 100-year-old doll.

- Bad luck and misfortune will fall upon anyone who dares visit and photograph the odd looking doll.

History

1900 – Robert Eugene Otto was born in Key West. He lived at 524 Eaton Street.

1904 – Four-year-old Robert was given a three-foot-tall straw doll. The doll was an effigy of the boy. It is believed that the doll came from the Haitian or Bohemian girl that was raised by Robert's parents. The boy named the doll "Robert" and began to refer to himself as "Gene."

1974 – Gene died. He was a well-known Key West artist.

1974 – Gene's wife moved back to her home town in Massachusetts, and the house was sold to Myrtle and William Reuter, and of course Robert the doll came with it.

1994 – Nancy Tazwell donated Robert to the East Martello Museum.

Currently – Robert rest in a glass case at the museum where he is open to viewing from the public.

Source: Key West Art & Historical Society

Investigation

Robert the Doll was given to young Gene as a present. While growing up, like most kids, Gene would get into trouble. However, every time something went wrong Gene would blame it on the doll saying, "Robert did it." Throughout his life Gene kept a close bond with Robert and even gave the doll its own room overlooking the street. In his later years Gene was often very abusive to his wife. Gene would often burst into fits of rage and then suddenly snap out of it and say that it was all Robert's fault.

One of the theories is that Robert was given to Gene by a Bohemian or Haitian woman that had put a voodoo spell on the doll.

The Mayor of Key West proclaimed that October 24th, 2004 was officially Robert the Enchanted Doll Day.

Robert the Doll has become so well-known that he even received a birthday card from President George W. Bush.

A volunteer informed us that often times he would be in the museum by himself closing up when he would hear the mysterious sounds of footsteps behind him. Thinking that someone was still in the building from a tour, the man searched the entire place, yet he never found anyone else in the building.

Several staff members told us that many unexplained events take place in the museum. It is common for people to see mysterious shadows move throughout the building. Many staff report hearing bizarre noises while alone in the museum, and those who are brave enough to search for an explanation never find one.

One gentleman claims that while he toured the building he snapped numerous photos of the antiques in the fort. As he was leaving, he took a few final photos of Robert. Once the photos were developed, the man was mystified because every single photo from the fort was of Robert.

It is reported that Robert has been known to tap on the glass when no one is watching and that he frequently moves his toy around the glass enclosure.

Perhaps the most bizarre report about Robert originates from those who claim that the doll's facial features will actually change depending on those who are present. The most common report is that Robert looks "evil," and is also believed that over the years Robert's face has changed along with his appearance.

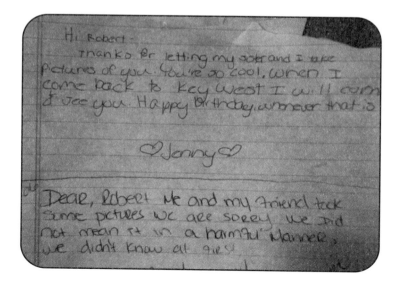

The Dare. If you take a picture of Robert, unavoidable bad luck will follow you. The wall behind Robert is filled with letters from previous visitors who tell of their misfortune after taking a picture of Robert. From lost luggage and speeding tickets to those who claim Robert broke their expensive cameras, tales of ill fortune serve as your warning.

(For more on Robert see "The Artist House.")

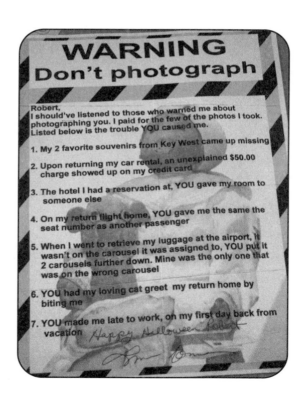

Restlawn Memorial Gardens

Location: Port Charlotte, Charlotte County, Florida
Address: Restlawn Memorial Garden Cemetery, 1380 Forrest Nelson Boulevard, Port Charlotte, FL 33952-2126

Directions: To the Cemetery: From Port Charlotte head north on Highway 41 (Tamiami Trail). Take a right on Forrest Nelson Blvd. Follow the boulevard and the cemetery will be on your right side.

To the home: Just before the cemetery is the address of 1416 on the right side of the road. Just before that address there is an unmarked dirt road (right across from 1515). Pull in the dirt road and park. Walk straight ahead and you will come to the broken bee pallets. Go to your right and cross the barbed wire fence. Follow the trail to the left until you reach the old house (Approx. 30 yards).

Ghost Lore

Years ago a farmer and his wife lived in the town's first home which was located right next to the land that the cemetery now occupies. The farmer went crazy and murdered his wife. After the murder the home sat empty. Little by little the years started to take their toll on the old home, and eventually the city had to condemn the dilapidated building.

- Phantom swarms of killer bees haunt the area and have terrorized the neighborhood for many years.

- At night an unknown ghostly figure has been seen walking throughout the cemetery.

- Mysterious noises can be heard coming from the former home of the murderous farmer.

History

1959 – The cemetery land was deeded.

1985 – The cemetery was purchased by the current owners.

1990s – The cemetery added another 20 acres to the grounds. An additional 30 acres of cemetery land remained undeveloped.

Investigation

The home where the farmer was said to have killed his wife is still standing. It is owned by a woman who also owns other property in the area. For the last few years the old building has been "occupied" by a homeless person.

We are unsure as to the history of the house itself. We do know that it was not the first house in Port Charlotte. We have been unable to find a story of a farmer killing his wife in the home.

We spoke with the man staying/squatting in the home and he told us that on many nights he will hear strange noises from the house. He felt that it was an eerie place to stay. It should be noted that many people walk around at night in the nearby wooded area trying to locate the home.

For years neighbors have reported being plagued by swarms of phantom bees. However, upon our investigation we found that right outside of the old house sits the discarded plywood bottoms from a bee farm that was once in operation there. A few years ago dozens of boxes of bees were housed at the bee farm, which may explain why the neighborhood has had so many bee problems.

At night many residents and visitors have reported seeing an unknown figure walking around inside the cemetery. Many people speculate that the figure is the ghost of the farmer or his murdered wife, yet no one is sure as to who or what this strange figure is . . . but "it" is most often seen at night.

Renaissance Vinoy Resort and Golf Club Hotel

Location: Saint Petersburg, Pinellas County, Florida
Address: 501 Fifth Avenue Northeast,
Saint Petersburg, FL 33701-2620
Phone: (727) 894-1000
Toll-Free: 1-888-303-4430
Fax: (727) 822-2785
Website: www.marriott.com/hotels/travel/tpasr-renaissance-vinoy-resort-and-golf-club/

Directions: From 375 go east on 4th Ave N toward the beach. Turn left on Beach Dr. NE. Turn right on 5th Ave. NE.

Ghost Lore

The elegant 1920s Vinoy Hotel proudly stands today as a constant reminder of a time long since past. From the moment you walk through the grand main doors of the hotel you can almost imagine hearing the sounds of a big band playing as dolled up flapper girls and men in fancy zoot suits dance the night away. Yet if you venture up to the fifth floor you may not have to imagine the past, you might just come face to face with it. Professional baseball players staying at the hotel were plagued by so many paranormal events that they vowed never to return.

- A spectral woman in white roams the 5th floor of the hotel.

- A mysterious spirit of a man in a top hat wanders the hotel at night.

History

1923 – Aymer Vinoy Laughner purchased the vacant land for the price of $170,000.

1925 – Architect Henry Taylor began construction on the grand hotel. Taylor guaranteed that he would finish the hotel by the end of the year.

1925 – On December 31, the Vinoy Park Hotel opened to the public. The nightly rate was $20 per room, which at the time was one of the most expensive room rates in the entire state.

1942 – The hotel resort was closed down and the building was leased to the US War Department.

1944 – After the end of the war the government cancelled their agreement with the Vinoy.

1945 – The hotel was purchased by Chicago businessman Charles Albering for $700,000.

1975 – Once again the hotel closed down. Prices had dropped from $50 a night to just $7, yet the hotel was unable to stay open.

1978 – Even thought the hotel had been closed for several years, it was placed on the National Register of Historic Places.

1980s – The hotel sat empty for several years. A group of concerned citizens began a movement to save the hotel from destruction.

1989 – Federal Construction Company was awarded a $33.6 million contract to renovate the Vinoy. Renovation plans also included expanding the Vinoy.

1992 – The Stouffer Vinoy Resort re-opens. The final cost of the renovation was nearly $100 million.

1996 – The hotel was purchased by CTF Hotels out of Hong Kong. The company added the name of "Renaissance" to the hotel.

1997 – Marriott International purchased the hotel from CTF Hotels.

2002 – The hotel underwent a $4 million restoration of all rooms.

Currently – The hotel is open to the public.

Source: Renaissance Vinoy Resort and Golf Club

Investigation

For years visiting professional baseball teams have stayed at the Vinoy while in town to play Tampa. A lot of mysterious happenings at the hotel have been experienced by these players.

While the Red Sox were staying at the hotel, a few of their players had some bizarre experiences in their room. The *Boston Globe* reported that Scott Williamson was awakened in middle of the night by a strange spirit pressing on his back. Williamson stated that he was lying on his stomach when all of a sudden he felt like he could not breathe. He quickly turned around only to see the spirit of a man dressed in 1920s style clothing standing over him.

Another player reported that while staying at the hotel he had some dry cleaning delivered to his room. He hung up the clothes and left the room for a short moment and when he returned, he was puzzled to find that his clothes were scattered all over his bed.

Two other players staying at the hotel complained that throughout the night the toilet in their bathroom keep being flushed by some unseen force.

The hotel has gained such a haunted reputation that a few years ago, when the Pittsburg Pirates came to town, several of the players refused to spend the evening at the hotel and stayed with a teammate's family that resided in the area instead.

A woman dressed in white is often seen roaming the fifth floor. Several historians speculate that it could be the murdered wife of a former hotel partner.

Most of the staff we spoke with were familiar with the legends and stories of the hotel. However, they were hesitant to share their stories.

Harder Hall

Location: Sebring, Highlands County, Florida
Address: 3300 Golfview Road, Sebring, FL 33875-5004

Directions: Drive west on Hammock Rd. (634), turn left on Lakewood Rd. Follow this to Golfview Rd., turn left, and the building is straight ahead.

Ghost Lore

At first glance, this magnificent hotel looks like a perfect paradise for tourists. Upon closer inspection, the hotel seems to be plagued with never-ending financial difficulties. Yet others believe that the historic hotel is plagued with suicides, murders, and the mysterious deaths of its owners.

- Mysterious music can be heard coming from the closed-down hotel.

- Security guards often chase phantom intruders through the building.

History

1925 – The Sebring White Way newspaper reported that a 1.5-million-dollar hotel was being financed by the Biltmore Hotel interests on a piece of land owned by Vincent Hall.

1925 – Hall reported that the new hotel would be named Lakewood Terrace. His partners were Lewis Harder and George Kline.

1925 – The name of the hotel was switched to Harder Hall in honor of Vincent Hall and Lewis Harder.

1926 – The grand hotel was slated to be completed, but instead the project was plagued with delays, budget problems, and financial failure which forced the company to seek bankruptcy.

1927 – Vincent Hall announced that he had secured new financing

for the project. Work began again on the previously stalled project. In order to curb skyrocketing costs, the original building design was cut back.

1928 – Harder Hall was completed. The finished building contained six floors of elegant guest rooms and even had an observation tower on the seventh floor.

1953 – Victor and David Jacobson, along with several other business partners, purchased the property.

1981 – The hotel was sold to a group of investors who failed to convert the property into privately-owned apartments.

1986 – The hotel building closed down, sat empty, and began to deteriorate.

1990 – The property was listed on the National Register of Historic Places.

1994 – Avi Limor purchased the hotel and invested over $1.5 million in it.

1995 – Mr. Limor died in a plane crash.

2003 – Avi Limor's widow sold the building to the Florida investor group of Joran Realty Corporation. They planned to re-open the hotel and began renovations to bring the building back to its origin grandeur.

2006 – Renovation on the building ceased as the project ran out of money.

2007 – The hotel and grounds were purchased by the city of Sebring.

Currently – The hotel and property are for sale. The city of Sebring is looking to sell the place for a reported $5.5 million.

Source: *Sebring City on the Circle* by Stephen Olausen

Investigation

The hotel has a long history of haunting activity. Stories of weird happenings date back to at least the 1940s.

Over the years, both guests and staff have reported hearing mysterious music coming from the hotel. Even after the hotel was closed down and vacant, the unexplained music still persisted.

People driving by the old closed-down hotel often report looking up into some of the hotel's windows and seeing the ghostly image of someone staring back at them.

We spoke with a security guard working at the property who informed us that she had experienced many strange events. One of the duties of the guard is to make rounds inside the building to be certain no intruders have broken in. She told us that on many nights she would be startled by a strange sound coming from one of the rooms, but upon investigation, no source for the noise could ever be found. On other nights, the guard would hear someone talking inside the building, but a search of the building turned up nothing.

Locals tell tales of the hotel being plagued with mysterious deaths and suicides. Our investigations uncovered at least one owner, Avi Limor, who died in a bizarre accident, but we are still trying to document other deaths or suicides that might have taken place in the hotel.

David Falk Theatre

Location: Tampa, Hillsborough County, Florida
Address: David Falk Theatre, 428 West Kennedy Boulevard, Tampa, FL 33606

Directions: Follow W. John F. Kennedy Blvd., and you will see the theatre on your right.

Ghost Lore

During the 1920s the theatre hosted various traveling Vaudeville performers. It was during this time that actress Bessie Snavely arrived in town with her fellow actors. The theatre was ripe with gossip that Bessie's husband was having relations with a young female stagehand. Once Bessie found out about the affair she quickly hatched a plan to murder them both. However, the heart-broken woman quickly changed her mind and decided that it would be much easier to take just one life—her own. In the third floor dressing room, Bessie gave one last performance as she took a rope and tied it tightly around her neck and ended her life. To this day Bessie roams the theatre that finished her career.

- The spirit of Bessie tries to prevent any leading lady from wearing the color red while performing on stage. Red was Bessie's favorite color to perform in.

- Bessie's spirit relentlessly roams the theatre, desperately searching for her cheating husband.

History

1928 – The Park Theatre was opened as both a vaudeville and movie theatre.

1932 to 1933 – The theatre changed its focus from live theater and started showing movies.

1940s – The property was operated by E. J. Sparks, a subsidiary of Paramount Pictures.

1962 – The University of Tampa took ownership of the theatre. The theatre was renamed the David Falk Memorial Theatre.

1981 – The theatre was closed down for extensive renovation and remodeling.

1981 – After being closed for nine months, the theatre re-opened with a production of the Nutcracker.

1992 to 1999 – The theatre served as the Stageworks in Residence.

Currently – The theatre is used exclusively by the University of Tampa's Department of Speech, Theatre, and Dance.

Source: University of Tampa

Investigation

Since the 1930s theatre staff and visitors have whispered about the story of the theatre being haunted by an actress named Bessie Snavely. The main version of the story states that Bessie did indeed find out about her husband's indiscretions and hanged herself at the end of a rope in her dressing room on the third floor. However, no one remembers the real origins of the story and no documentation of the death of an actress has been produced.

Another less-told version of the legend states that Bessie was deeply in love with one the stage hands that traveled with her group. The legend states that although Bessie's infatuation was well-known, is was not reciprocated. Facing the pain of rejection, Bessie decided that her heart simply could not bear the thought of not being with her one true love. Heartbroken, Bessie then committed suicide in her third floor dressing room.

Jack Powell, in his book *Haunted Sunshine,* wrote of a staff member who was in the theatre when he heard noises coming from outside his office. The man got up to check out the odd sounds and as soon as he opened the door the noises immediately stopped, and the man was left staring at a shapeless cloud of white mist that quickly disappeared into the wall.

Throughout the years, dozens of stage performers and workers had experienced terrifying encounters with the heartbroken spirit of Bessie Snavely. For years, workers have tried their hardest to avoid Bessie's old dressing room. Those who absolutely have to visit the room often report being covered in an eerie coldness that could not be explained.

We spoke with several staff members who informed us that numerous people who work late nights inside the theatre have felt an uneasy sense that they are not alone. On several occasions, workers have seen a transparent image of a woman believed to be Bessie floating around the theatre. Due to the creepy nature of these sightings many workers simply refuse to be alone in the theatre at night.

Myrtle Hill Memorial Park

Location: Tampa, Hillsborough County, Florida
Address: 4207 East Lake Avenue, Tampa, FL 33610-8035

Directions: From 275 North turn right onto E. Dr. Martin
Luther King Jr. Blvd. (574). Turn right on N. 42nd St. Turn on
East Lake Street.

Ghost Lore

When you first arrive at the cemetery you immediately notice the
large stone walls and white gate that together pose an intimidating
barrier for those looking to enter the graveyard. However, you
soon may realize that maybe the gates were not meant to simply
keep out nighttime trespassers, but instead they keep in the spirits
of the cemetery. Because hidden deep inside this expansive cemetery sits not only a haunted mausoleum but also numerous paranormal anomalies.

- The smell of rotten flesh permeates throughout the cemetery.

- The cemetery is plagued by the mysterious sounds of women yelling and screaming.

History

1917 – The 105-acre cemetery was founded by Daniel Wells, T. O. Wilson, and Clifton Benson.

1926 – A new Catholic section was added to the cemetery due to the closing of another local Catholic cemetery. Approximately 100 bodies were moved from the old cemetery to Myrtle Hill.

1932 – The cemetery was purchased by A. C. Clewis and George Howel.

1960s – A garden mausoleum and chapel were constructed on the cemetery grounds.

Investigation

In his book *Florida's Ghostly Legends and Haunted Folklore*, Greg Jenkins writes of his investigation into the cemetery. Once inside the cemetery, Jenkins and a friend were drawn to a mausoleum. When they positioned themselves in front of the door they were immediately overcome with a sense of dread, and then a gust of a rancid smelling air rushed upon them. The cemetery provided little light, but it was just enough to cast shadows of something moving inside the mausoleum. Accompanying the shadows were the soft sounds of someone whispering. Thinking that someone was squatting in the cemetery, they left the mausoleum and watched the opening to see the people come out. However, no one exited the mausoleum.

Many locals tell stories of hearing the sounds of women inside the cemetery crying out for help. Concerned residents have approached the cemetery to determine the crisis and were unable to find the source of the spectral screams for help.

Several investigative teams have set out to investigate the cemetery. Most groups report capturing audio recordings of unknown voices (EVPs) during their investigations.

The Dare. If you walk into any of the cemetery's mausoleums, you will disturb the spirits and they will make themselves known to you.

Tampa Theatre

Location: Tampa, Hillsborough County, Florida
Address: 711 North Franklin Street,Tampa, FL 33602-4435

Directions: Head northwest on North Ashley Dr. Turn right on E. Zack St. Turn left on N. Franklin Street, and you will see the theatre.

Ghost Lore

In today's ever changing business world, job security and employee loyalty seem like concepts from a forgotten era. Long gone are the days in which employees spend their entire career with one organization, only to retire with a golden watch. However, history shows us that in generations past most people often spent their entire lives working at one place. Foster "Fink" Finley seems to have gone above and beyond his fellow workers, because not only did Fink spend over 35 years working at the theatre, he has even spent his afterlife working there as well.

- A phantom projectionist ensures that the theatre continues to run without a hitch.

- On many occasions an unknown apparition has been spotted floating in front of the screen.

History

1926 – The theatre was designed by architect John Eberson and constructed at a cost of over $1.2 million.

1926 – The theatre opened with the silent movie *The Ace of Cards*.

1960s – Theatre audiences began to wane, putting the theatre in danger of folding under.

1965 – Foster "Fink" Finley suffered heart pain and was taken from the theatre and died.

1973 – Due to ongoing struggles with finances the theatre finally closed down.

1976 – The theatre was acquired by the City of Tampa. Extensive renovation of the theatre began to restore it to its original glory, thus saving the theatre from being torn down.

1977 – The theatre was added to the National Register of Historic Places.

1978 – The theatre re-opened under the supervision of The Arts Council of Hillsborough.

1988 – The building was declared a Tampa City Landmark.

Source: Tampa Theatre

Investigation

Foster "Fink" Finley was an employee at the Tampa Theatre for most of his life. He worked mainly as a projectionist, yet Fink was often the first to volunteer when other jobs needed to be done around the theatre. One day in 1965, Fink was hit with severe chest pains. The pain was so extreme that Fink had to be driven home by a co-worker. Two months later Fink was dead.

After Fink's death things eventually returned back to normal around the theatre. The struggle to keep the business afloat occupied most of the employees' time and energy. However, things were about to change as the theatre underwent major renovations. It is believed that the constant construction not only put an end to the normalcy but that it also awakened the ghostly spirit of Fink.

A *St. Petersburg Times* article reported that weird occurrences began sometime in the late 1960s when staff began to hear keys jingling and other bizarre noises that they could not explain.

Dan Asfar, in his book, *Ghost Stories of Florida,* wrote that employees would often report that their personal items would come up missing, only to be found in the most unusual places.

Rose Historical Cemetery

Location: Tarpon Springs, Pinellas County, Florida
Address: North Jasmine Avenue and East Orange Street,
Tarpon Springs, FL 34689

Directions: Head east on East Tarpon Ave. and turn left on N.
Jasmine Ave. The cemetery will be on your left. It sits one
block away from the much larger Cycadia Cemetery.

Ghost Lore

In the days of segregation, African Americans were not allowed to
be buried inside the "white" cemeteries. Rose Hill Cemetery was
created to provide a final resting place for many of the community's African Americans. Yet, because only 20% of the bodies in the
cemetery were outfitted with a proper burial and tombstone, their
troubled spirits failed to rest.

- At night the spirits of the unknown people walk through the cemetery waiting for a proper burial.

- Those who visit the cemetery are immediately overcome with a strong sense of dread.

History

1904 – The first burial took place inside the cemetery. However, many researchers have found evidence that burials took place on the land prior to 1904.

1916 – The cemetery was deeded to a community board of citizens. The five original members were Florence White, Mahala Jones, Susie Holman, Matilda Castro and Mahala Perry. The group was given a 99-year lease on the property.

1917 – The property was officially deeded to the association.

1949 – The trustees of the Internal Improvement Fund of the State of Florida deeded several more land lots to be used as the cemetery expanded. The transaction was signed by Governor Fuller Warren.

1953 – The City of Tarpon Springs deeded addition lots to Rose Cemetery.

1978 – An attorney, Mr. Hilbert Elliot, helped with the legal process of setting up the non-profit organization called Rose Hill Cemetery.

1979 – The second board of directors was set up during a meeting at the Mount Moriah Church.

1979 – The name of Rose Hill Cemetery was officially changed to the Rose Cemetery Association.

1998 – The cemetery was awarded a 501-c3 status as a non-profit organization.

2003 – The cemetery was listed as a Florida State Historical Site.

2005 – The seventy-five-year-old caretaker reached out to the community to provide a hand in the maintenance of the historic cemetery.

2008 – The cemetery continued to work to receive national recognition as a historic cemetery.

Source: Rose Cemetery

Investigation

The cemetery has about 600 marked graves. Researchers believe as many as 1,400 additional people lie in unidentified and unmarked graves.

The fact that the cemetery is overrun with unmarked graves has given rise to the local legend of the haunted graveyard. It is said that the unhappy spirits of the cemetery's unknown inhabitants are upset over being forgotten, and they walk the grounds wanting to be recognized.

During an investigation of the cemetery, a paranormal group claimed to have recorded a mysterious unknown voice on audio (EVP) while inside the cemetery.

This case is pending.

Bloody Bucket Bridge

Location: Wauchula, Hardee County, Florida

Directions: Head east on Main St. Approximately one mile down the road you will come to Bridge Road (In front of Circle K store). Turn right and follow this to the Bloody Bucket Bridge.

Ghost Lore

Do you remember the old game show *Let's Make a Deal*? You know, the show where the contestants could choose one of three curtains and win whatever prizes were behind them. Well this ghost lore is like that old game show, because there are three different versions of the origin of the haunting. Door number 1: Bloody Bucket Bridge is haunted by the spirit of a deranged midwife who, instead of helping deliver babies, murdered them. Door number 2: The place is haunted by the restless spirits of men who were stabbed and shot to death at a nearby saloon called Bloody Bucket Bar. Door number 3: The Bridge is haunted by the angry spirits of the African American men who were lynched and hanged on the old bridge.

- The river will turn red with the blood of murdered children.
- The ghostly cries of children can be heard coming from the river.

History

The history of the bridge is unknown.

Investigation

Even though everyone in town seemed to know the legend of Bloody Bucket Bridge, their versions of the stories varied greatly.

The most sinister version of the story revolves around a former Georgia slave who years ago traveled down to Florida. The woman was said to be an excellent midwife who proudly bragged about delivering over 200 babies. Local folks were only too happy to have her assistance until their babies started dying at birth. The townspeople suspected that the midwife was actually smothering their babies and burying the remains down by the river. Although they had no proof of her crimes, families stopped using the midwife, and slowly the old woman lost her mind. Consumed with guilt and possessing a shattered mind, the woman believed that her buckets would fill up with the blood of the murdered babies. The woman would spend her days walking to the bridge to empty her bloody buckets into the river. One day the old woman slipped and fell into the river and drowned. For several days after her death, the locals reported that the river had turned blood red.

We found no evidence to support this version of the legend, and it appears that the story was created by a local writer in 2003. Although the story is not true, people are still having experiences associated with this story (see below).

We spoke with two men who often go fishing down at the river. They said that on one occasion the water seemed to turn red right before their eyes. The scared men tried to laugh it off and blame it on the tannic acid from the shoreline trees, yet they still quickly packed up their gear and headed home.

A young woman told us that one evening she drove out to the bridge with a group of her friends to check out the bloody legend. Once they arrived at the bridge, they walked down to the banks of the river where they heard the eerie sound of babies crying. The group was puzzled to find that they were unable to find where the mysterious sounds were coming from and decided it best just to leave.

Another version of the legend tells that many years ago the bridge was the spot where locals lynched and hanged several African Americans. It is believed that their spirits still roam the bridge looking for revenge on their murderers. We were also unable to find any evidence of this version. However, that is not to say that the hangings and lynching never happened.

The third version of the legend seems to have the most credibility to it. This story goes that years ago there was a bar located across the road from the bridge. The bar was a seedy and dangerous place that attracted a rowdy crowd. The bar got the nickname of "Bloody Bucket Bar" due to the numerous stabbings and killings that took place at the saloon.

We spoke with several local historians and residents who recalled that a bar did exist out next to the bridge, and it did indeed have a tainted reputation. It is believed that the bar was still in operation into the late 1940s. No one can remember the bar's name or the person who owned it.

About the Authors

Chad Lewis is a paranormal investigator for Unexplained Research LLC, with a Master's Degree in Applied Psychology from the University of Wisconsin-Stout. Chad has spent years traveling the globe researching ghosts, strange creatures, crop formations, and UFOs. Chad is a former state director for the Mutual UFO Network and has worked with BLT Research on crop circle investigations. Chad is the organizer of the *Unexplained* Conferences and hosted *The Unexplained* paranormal radio talk show and television series.

Terry Fisk is also a paranormal investigator for Unexplained Research LLC and lecturer on death and the afterlife. He is a shamanic Buddhist practitioner and member of the Foundation for Shamanic Studies who studied Philosophy and Religion at the University of Wisconsin. Terry co-hosted *The Unexplained* paranormal radio talk show and directed *The Unexplained* television series. He has investigated hauntings with famed medium Allison DuBois and TV psychic Chip Coffey.

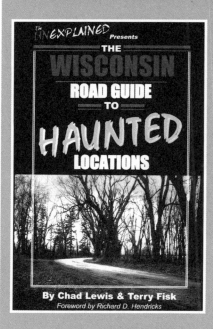

Wisconsin
Road Guide to Haunted Locations
by Chad Lewis & Terry Fisk
Foreword by Richard D. Hendricks

Where to go to possibly . . .
- *Be chased by hellhounds*
- *See statues come to life*
- *Go camping with ghosts*
- *Pick up a vanishing hitchhiker*
- *Sleep in a haunted bed & breakfast*
- *Worship with a phantom church*
- *Look into the portal to hell*
- *Chase phantom chickens*

ISBN: *978-0-9762099-1-1*

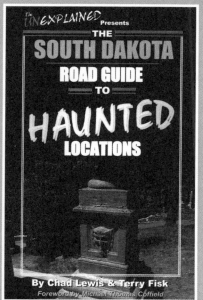

South Dakota
Road Guide to Haunted Locations
by Chad Lewis & Terry Fisk
Foreword by Michael Thomas Coffield

Where to go to possibly . . .
- *See the apparition of Seth Bullock*
- *Eat, drink, and gamble with phantoms*
- *Observe objects moving on their own*
- *Visit a haunted theater*
- *Hear ghostly wails in the Badlands*
- *Sleep in a haunted historic hotel*
- *Find the ghosts of Ma and Pa Ingalls*
- *Encounter the ghost of Jesse James*

ISBN: *978-0-9762099-3-5*

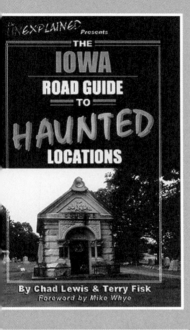
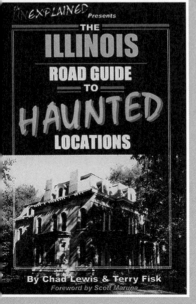

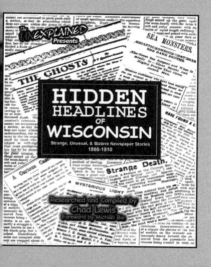
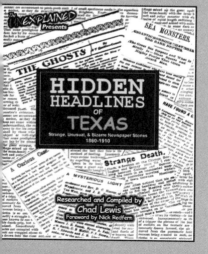

Unexplained Research LLC
P.O. Box 2173
Eau Claire, WI 54702-2173
www.unexplainedresearch.com
admin@unexplainedresearch.com